CW01313033

SCIENCE FOR EXCELLENC

LEVEL 4

biological science

Scottish Schools Science Group

Series Editors:
Nicky Souter, Paul Chambers and Stephen Jeffrey

Authors:
Nicky Souter, Pat Carney, Karen Parker
and Robert Rowney

DYNAMIC LEARNING

HODDER GIBSON
AN HACHETTE UK COMPANY

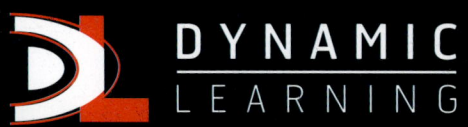

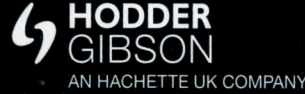

The Publishers would like to thank the following for permission to reproduce copyright material:
Photo credits
p.8 (top) © Michael Maloney/San Francisco Chronicle/Corbis; p.9 © Flirt Collection / Photolibrary; p.10 © Imagestate Media; p.11 © WALLY EBERHART, VISUALS UNLIMITED /SCIENCE PHOTO LIBRARY; p.12 © Ian Murray/LOOP IMAGES/Loop Images/Corbis; p.13 (top left) © NASA, (middle right) © Eye Ubiquitous / Alamy; p.14 © Reuters/CORBIS; p.15 (top) © Tim Laman / Getty Images, (middle) © Z1022/_Patrick Pleul/dpa/Corbis, (bottom) © vchphoto / Fotolia.com; p.18 ©Photodisc/Getty Images; p.21 (bottom) © Chinch Gryniewicz; Ecoscene/CORBIS; p.23 (right) © Ned Therrien/Visuals Unlimited/Corbis; p.24 (top) © Imagestate Media; p.25 (top) © Garden Picture Library / Getty Images, (middle) © Sandra Cunningham / Fotolia.com, (bottom right) © Nigel Cattlin / Alamy; p.26 (top) © Elke Borkowski / GAP Photos, (bottom) © Jacqui Dracup / Garden World Images; p.30 © Inmagine / Alamy; p.36 NASA Goddard Space Flight Center (NASA-GSFC); p.38 (left) © Stockbyte/ Photolibrary Group Ltd, (middle from top) © CSeigneurgens - Fotolia.com, © auris – Fotolia, © iStockphoto.com/ sweetym, (right from top) © Ashley Whitworth – Fotolia, ©Milos Luzanin/istockphoto.com, © Fatman73 – Fotolia; p.39 © Tino Soriano/National Geographic Society/Corbis; p.40 (top left) © Gail Johnson – Fotolia, (top right) © Syngas, (bottom right) © AVTG/istockphoto.com; p.42 (top) © The Woodland Trust; p.45 (top) © Chris Pearsall / Alamy, (middle left) © Joe Gough / Fotolia.com, (middle right) © Beepstock / Alamy; p.46 ©Photodisc/Getty Images; p.47 (top) © Chris Howes/Wild Places Photography / Alamy, (bottom) © Imagestate Media; p.48 © Gari Wyn Williams / Alamy; p.49 © PASIEKA/SCIENCE PHOTO LIBRARY; p.50 ©Photodisc/Getty Images; p.52 (top left) © Balfour Studios / Alamy, (top right) © Melking – Fotolia, (bottom) © imagebroker / Alamy; p.53 (top left) ©Photodisc/ Photolibrary Group Ltd, (top right) © Gary Crabbe / Alamy; p.55 (top) © Imagestate Media, (middle) © Ben Hall / Getty Images, (bottom) © blickwinkel / Alamy; p.56 (top) © Imagestate Media, (bottom) © Editorial / Alamy; p.59 ©Photodisc/Getty Images; p.60 © HYBRID MEDICAL ANIMATION / SCIENCE PHOTO LIBRARY; p.61 ©Photodisc/Getty Images; p.62 (top) © Peter Dazeley / Getty Images, (bottom right) © Dennis Kunkel Microscopy, Inc./Visuals Unlimited/Corbis; p.63 (left) © PCN/Corbis, (right) © Adam Gault / Getty Images; p.66 © POWER AND SYRED/SCIENCE PHOTO LIBRARY; p.73 (top) © SCIENCE PHOTO LIBRARY; p.74 (right) © Carolina Biological/Visuals Unlimited/Corbis; p.76 © Visuals Unlimited/Corbis; p.79 (top) © Russi & Morelli – Fotolia; p.80 (top) © Stockbyte/Getty Images, (bottom) © Eddie Gerald / Alamy; p.82 (top) © Monika Adamczyk - Fotolia.com, (bottom) © DLILLC/Corbis; p.83 © MICHAEL ABBEY/SCIENCE PHOTO LIBRARY; p.85 © The James Hutton Institute; p.86 (top) © Tetra Images / Alamy, (bottom) © c.20thC.Fox/Everett/Rex Features; p.87 © CDC/PHIL/CORBIS; p.89 (top from left) ©Nigel Monckton – Fotolia, © Tetra Images/Corbis, (bottom from left) ©Photodisc/Getty Images, ©Grafvision – Fotolia; p.91 (top) ©Steven Paine – Fotolia, (bottom) ©Photodisc/Getty Images; p.92 © JOHN BAVOSI/SCIENCE PHOTO LIBRARY; p.94 (left) © POWER AND SYRED / SCIENCE PHOTO LIBRARY, (right) © PEGGY GREB/US DEPARTMENT OF AGRICULTURE/SCIENCE PHOTO LIBRARY; p.95 (top) ©Andrzej Tokarski – Fotolia, (bottom) © ZEPHYR/SCIENCE PHOTO LIBRARY. pp.6, 20, 28, 35 © Digital Stock. pp.44, 51, 58, 65, 72, 78 © Photodisc/Getty Images. p.88 © Photodisc/Getty Images. p.8 (middle and bottom), p.13 (middle left), p.16, p.19, p.21 (top), p.22, p.23 (left), p.24 (far left, middle left and bottom), p.25 (bottom left), p.31, p.40 (bottom left), p.41 (all), p.42 (bottom), p.53 (bottom), p.62 (bottom left), p.67, p.68, p.69 (all), p.73 (bottom), p.74 (left), p.79 (bottom), p.90, p.93 © Nicky Souter. Every effort has been made to trace all copyright holders, but if any have been inadvertently overlooked the Publishers will be pleased to make the necessary arrangements at the first opportunity.

Acknowledgement
The gene therapy artwork on p.70 is based on artwork by US National Library of Medicine.

Although every effort has been made to ensure that website addresses are correct at time of going to press, Hodder Gibson cannot be held responsible for the content of any website mentioned in this book. It is sometimes possible to find a relocated web page by typing in the address of the home page for a website in the URL window of your browser.

Hachette UK's policy is to use papers that are natural, renewable and recyclable products and made from wood grown in sustainable forests. The logging and manufacturing processes are expected to conform to the environmental regulations of the country of origin.

Whilst every effort has been made to check the intructions of practical work in this book, it is still the duty and legal obligation of schools to carry out their own risk assessment.

Orders: please contact Bookpoint Ltd, 130 Milton Park, Abingdon, Oxon OX14 4SB. Telephone: (44) 01235 827720.
Fax: (44) 01235 400454. Lines are open 9.00–5.00, Monday to Saturday, with a 24-hour message answering service. Visit our website at www.hoddereducation.co.uk. Hodder Gibson can be contacted direct on: Tel: 0141 848 1609; Fax: 0141 889 6315; email: hoddergibson@hodder.co.uk

© Scottish Schools Science Group 2011
First published in 2011 by
Hodder Gibson, an imprint of Hodder Education,
An Hachette UK Company
2a Christie Street
Paisley PA1 1NB

Impression number   5 4 3 2
Year   2014 2013

All rights reserved. Apart from any use permitted under UK copyright law, no part of this publication may be reproduced or transmitted in any form or by any means, electronic or mechanical, including photocopying and recording, or held within any information storage and retrieval system, without permission in writing from the publisher or under licence from the Copyright Licensing Agency Limited. Further details of such licences (for reprographic reproduction) may be obtained from the Copyright Licensing Agency Limited, Saffron House, 6–10 Kirby Street, London EC1N 8TS.

Cover photo © Nicky Souter
Illustrations by Emma Golley at Redmoor Design, Tony Wilkins, and DC Graphic Design Limited, Swanley, Kent
Typeset in Minion 12/15pt by DC Graphic Design Limited, Swanley, Kent
Printed in Dubai

A catalogue record for this title is available from the British Library

ISBN: 978 1444 145236

Contents

Introduction 4

1. It all depends on ... 6
2. Plant growth and reproduction 20
3. Investigating aerobic respiration 28
4. Saving the planet 35
5. Finding a perfect balance 44
6. Behave! 51
7. Cell growth and repair 58
8. Biotechnology 65
9. Reproduction and animal life cycles 72
10. Inheritance 78
11. Biochemistry 88

Index 97

Curriculum for Excellence mapping grid 100

Introduction

Science for Excellence Level 4: Biological Science is directed towards the Level Four Science experiences and outcomes of Curriculum for Excellence in Scotland. Its main focus is on those relating to life science in Planet Earth, Biological Systems and Materials. It makes frequent reference to key concepts identified in Curriculum for Excellence and the topics chosen in the text can be linked with content across the other organisers.

Although the chapters are designed to meet Curriculum for Excellence Level Four outcomes, their approach and content have also been influenced by the need to articulate with National Four and National Five developments which were underway at the time of writing. An enquiry-based approach suggests activities which are designed to encourage pupils to plan and design experiments which present opportunities for individual investigation or practical challenges but also others which are more designed to provide progression onto the next stage. This is reflected in the inclusion of content covering reproduction, cellular processing and inheritance, novel areas, such as behaviour for this stage, and homeostasis.

In an attempt to allow our pupils to make more informed decisions on scientific issues relating to their own experiences, the chapters have a strong Scottish viewpoint, but this is balanced by reference to global issues. It is hoped that the life science content, presented alongside examples of historical ideas, will develop pupils' awareness of science as a continuing process involving tentative ideas, and that what is considered correct at one time may be refined in light of new discoveries.

Some of the activities in the book involve experiments. These should only be attempted under the instruction of the Science Teacher and in accordance with the appropriate safety guidelines. Problems and activities are designed to examine and extend the content of the chapters. Skills in literacy and numeracy as well as an awareness of the importance of health and wellbeing will be developed through these exercises – look out for the icons shown at the end of this Introduction. Some chapters allow for numerical and graphical activities where others seek to reinforce the scientific principles contained in the main text. It was also felt that in an attempt to make the learners more active participants, open ended and pupil investigation activities should feature. These activities encourage individual project work, research and group work, with learners being asked to make informed decisions on scientific advances which may have ethical or societal implications. The tasks are designed around the 'broad features of assessment in science'.

The principles and practices outlined in Curriculum for Excellence have been adopted throughout the *Science for Excellence* series. The series is designed to be used in conjunction with schemes of work which reflect learning and teaching approaches which are most applicable to the sciences.

The series provides opportunities for scientific enquiry and examples of scientific scenarios where pupils can, for example, link variables to determine relationships or improve their scientific thinking or make informed judgements on the basis of scientific principles.

Introduction

Scientifically Literate Citizens

The series' use of real data and experimental type situations are designed to support the development of pupils' scientific attitudes. They will be able to look at data critically, make informed judgements on the basis of these and be critical and analytical of the science as well as the implications of broad or bold claims. Our scientific and technological development in various areas and at various times is recorded, and the impact of those developments is seen in context and as an indication of how our society has used and managed science for our benefit.

A significant challenge for Curriculum for Excellence and the *Science for Excellence* series is to change our pupils' attitudes to science and to help them become more able to engage positively in issues that will affect them. It is intended that the series' approach and content will help them to appreciate the scientific challenges and issues facing mankind and to respond in critical and informed ways. Enquiry, scepticism, analysis and questioning lie at the heart of 'real' science; we offer, in the text and within the selected images, some of the dilemmas facing science and society. These require continual revisiting and further scrutiny.

Science for Excellence strives to act as a sound preparatory text for all pupils, including those progressing to the next stage, providing a secure understanding of the key issues in science.

We are inspired by science and its impact on our lives. We have been motivated by the pupils and new teachers we have taught, our colleagues in schools. Teachers are, outside the family, the most important influence on young people; the quality of their work is frequently underestimated and *Science for Excellence* is offered to support their challenging work. We are grateful for the patience and constant support of the outstanding team at Hodder Gibson as well as those closest to us.

Nicky Souter, Paul Chambers and Stephen Jeffrey
Series Editors
Science for Excellence
2011

 Literacy

 Numeracy

 Health and Wellbeing

PLANET EARTH
Biodiversity and Interdependence

It all depends on ...

Level 3 — What came before?

 SCN 3-01a

I can sample and identify living things from different habitats to compare their biodiversity and can suggest reasons for their distribution.

 SCN 3-03a

Through investigations and based on experimental evidence, I can explain the use of different types of chemicals in agriculture and their alternatives and can evaluate their potential impact on the world's food production.

Level 4 — What is this chapter about?

 SCN 4-01a

I understand how animal and plant species depend on each other and how living things are adapted for survival. I can predict the impact of population growth and natural hazards on biodiversity.

 SCN 4-03a

Through investigating the nitrogen cycle and evaluating results from practical experiments I can suggest a design for a fertiliser, taking account of its environmental impact.

It all depends on ...

Food chains, food webs and interdependence

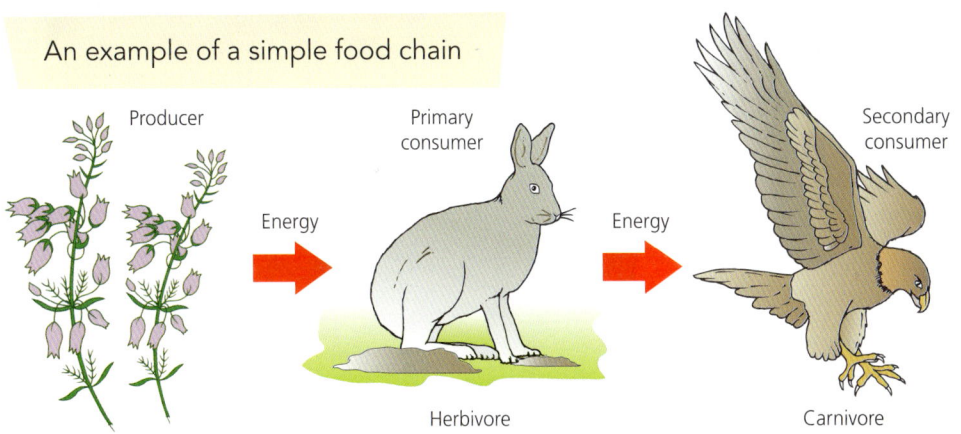

Food chains and food webs depend on energy flow between living things. They rely on plants converting light energy into chemical energy during **photosynthesis**. Once the chemical energy is stored in the plant, it may be passed on to herbivores. These primary consumers are eaten by carnivores, the secondary consumers, and some of the energy is passed on. All living things depend on at least one other to ensure their survival. Living things depend on each other. This is interdependence.

Food chains and food webs describe the interdependence of living things. The routes that energy takes when it passes through the ecosystem are indicated by arrows. Interdependence in living things occurs in other ways as well.

INTERDEPENDENCE

All members of an ecosystem are interconnected in a vast and intricate network of relationships, the web of life.

(Capra and Pauli (Eds)(1995). United Nations University Press)

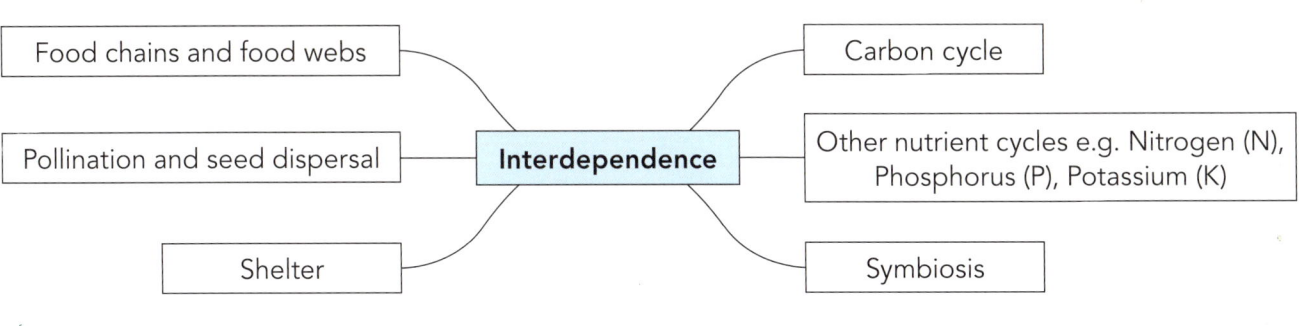

7

It all depends on ...

Interdependence – other examples

Pollination

The transfer of pollen from the male part of flowers (stamen) to the female part (carpel) results in fertilisation. This provides a new combination of genes which are transported in the seeds. Flowering plants often depend on animals to carry out pollination. Although bats, birds and mice are sometimes involved as pollinating agents, it is the insects that are most frequently involved in the pollination of flowering plants.

Pollinating animals are attracted to flowers by scent and nutritious nectar and pollen – these are their rewards for visiting the flower. Pollen sticks to their bodies and is transferred to other flowers and this results in pollination and fertilisation.

Insect pollination

Seed dispersal

Plants often depend on animals' coats to carry their seeds from one place to another.

Other plants depend on animals eating their fruits and spreading the seeds in their waste. While the fleshy part of a fruit is digested, the embryo is not because it is protected by a tough seed coat. Seeds pass out of the animal's body and are carried away. They pass out of the body at some distance from the parent plant in the **faeces** which provides fertiliser and water which assist germination of the seeds.

'Sticky willie' seeds and leaves stick to fur, feathers or clothing and are carried away from the parent plant.

Active Learning

Activity

Design an experiment to find out if the jelly affects tomato seed germination.

Tomato seeds fill the chambers inside a tomato fruit. Each seed is surrounded by jelly.

8

It all depends on ...

Interdependence – shelter

The variety of animals and plants which can live in any habitat depends on the climatic conditions and on other living things. Physical factors include light intensity, day length, temperature, minerals, pH and the availability of water. These are called **abiotic** factors. **Biotic** factors include the living things that are found there grazing or as predators as well as the influence of humankind.

Living things also depend on each other for shelter. They change the conditions around themselves and create a '**microclimate**'.

Have you ever sheltered from the weather beneath a large tree? How different is the temperature and the exposure to wind in particular?

Trees provide shelter for animals. The animals are protected from extreme environmental conditions and from predators. Trees also provide a place for birds to build their nests and provide food for huge numbers of insects and other organisms. Oaks support greater biodiversity than any other European tree. This dominant member of native woodland can be colonised by as many as 300 insect species.

Interdependence – carbon cycle

The carbon cycle also shows how living things depend on each other. **Aerobic respiration** depends on a constant supply of oxygen which is provided by photosynthesis which in turn depends on a constant supply of carbon dioxide (CO_2). Tomato growers often add CO_2 to the atmosphere in their greenhouses to boost fruit production.

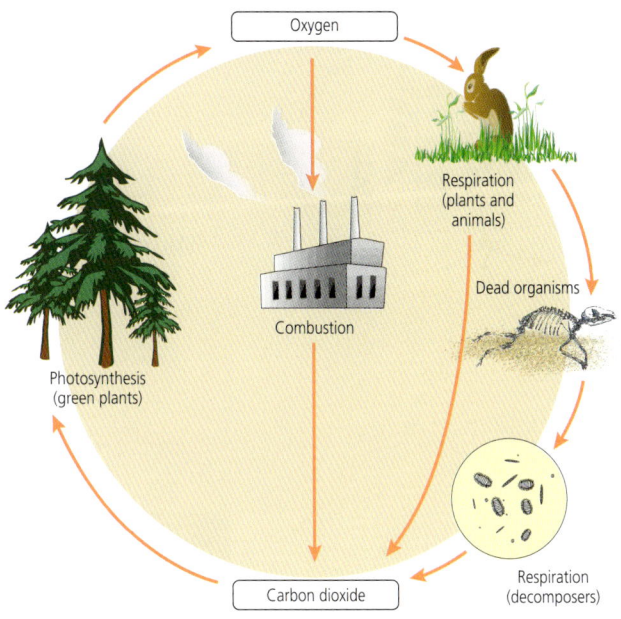

The carbon cycle

Disrupting the carbon cycle

The Earth's atmosphere includes 0.04% carbon dioxide. Rising CO_2 levels during the past 200 years have been linked to activities related to industrialisation and burning fossil fuels. At the same time rainforests are being cleared which reduces CO_2 removal by photosynthesis. Each of these is disrupting the carbon cycle.

It all depends on ...

Interdependence – other examples

Interdependence – other nutrient cycles

Living things depend on small masses of lots of different chemicals. Nutrients such as nitrogen, phosphorus, potassium and sulphur are essential. Physical processes, such as the dissolving of rock, and biological processes, such as decomposition, return these important chemicals to the environment. Nutrient cycles often involve micro-organisms.

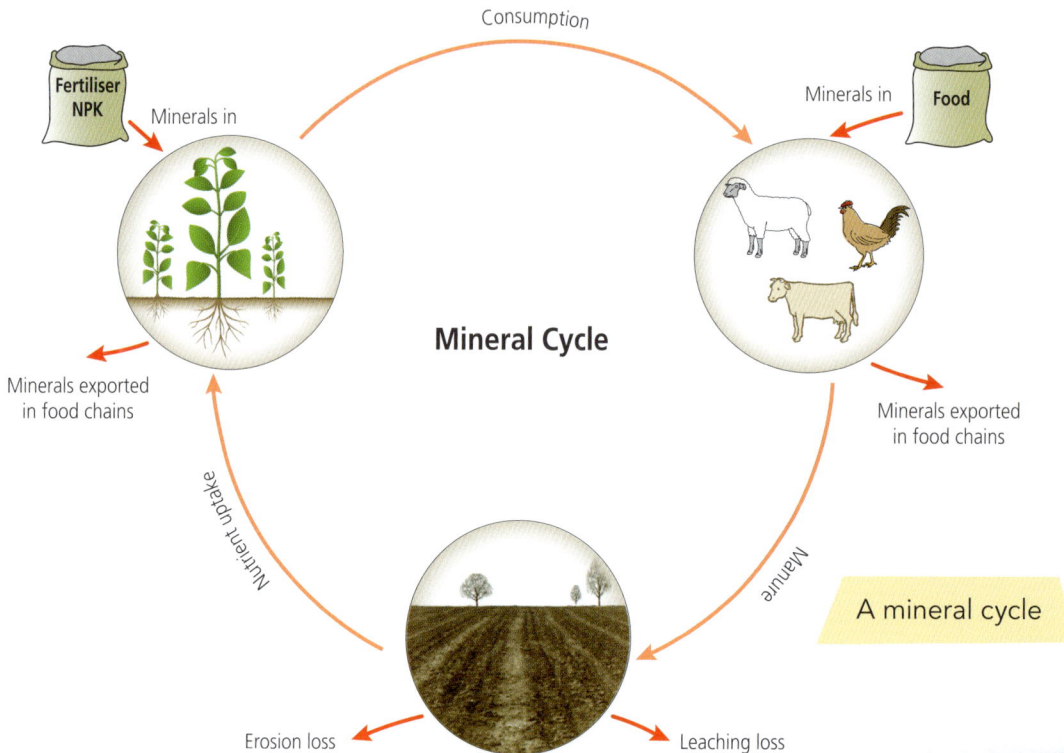

A mineral cycle

Decomposition

Some organisms, such as bacteria and fungi, actually feed on the dead remains of plants and animals and their waste. These organisms are given the name '**decomposers**' because they break down the compounds contained in plants and animals as they are feeding, releasing elements such as nitrogen back into the environment.

This toadstool is an example of a decomposer.

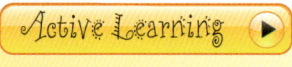

Activity

Leave an orange or piece of fruit to decompose completely. Make a photographic record of the changes that take place over several weeks.

It all depends on ...

Interdependence – the nitrogen cycle

The element nitrogen is recycled through all ecosystems. Nitrogen is essential to the survival and chemistry of all living things because it is found in all proteins and nucleic acids. The nitrogen cycle involves a series of chemical reactions that transfers nitrogen between the non-living environment and living things.

Several of the chemical reactions involved in the nitrogen cycle rely on bacteria.

contained in the roots of certain plants from the pea family – 'leguminous' plants.

Root nodules on a leguminous plant

Once nitrates enter plants they are turned into proteins and other useful chemicals. Nitrogen passes through food chains.

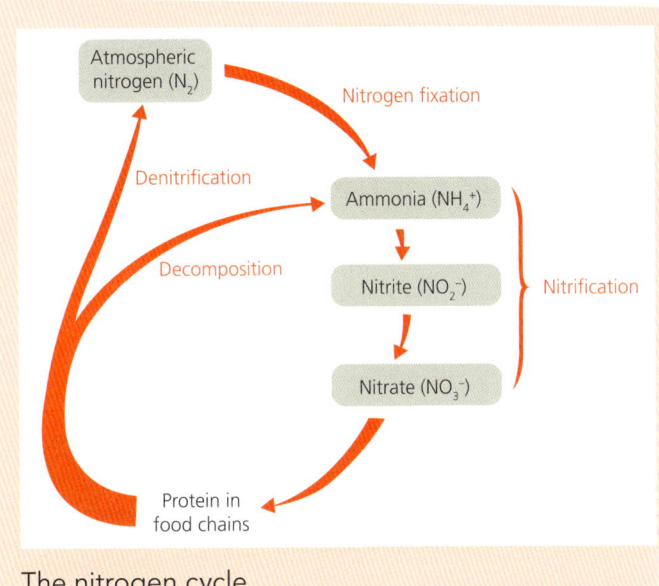

The nitrogen cycle

Nitrogen fixation

Atmospheric nitrogen is very stable. It takes a lot of energy to carry out the complicated chemical reactions that 'fix' or trap nitrogen. During storms, the massive amount of energy released by lightning enables nitrogen gas from the air to combine with water to form **nitrates**.

Nitrogen gas from the air can also be converted directly into nitrates through the action of **nitrogen-fixing bacteria**. These are found living in water or soil. They are also found in nodules

Decomposition

Animal waste, manure and urine, and the remains of dead plants and animals undergo a process of decay. Decomposer organisms, bacteria and fungi, digest the proteins and turn them into ammonia.

Nitrification

Ammonia is metabolised by **nitrifying bacteria** into **nitrites** and then into soluble nitrate. Plants absorb soluble nitrate along with other minerals from the environment through their roots. Plant cells convert the nitrate into **amino acids** which are then turned into proteins. The element nitrogen is then able to pass through food chains.

Denitrification

Excess nitrate in the soil is broken down into nitrogen gas by **denitrifying bacteria**. The nitrogen is then released back into the atmosphere.

Fertilisers and agriculture

Compost, decomposed material and manure have been added to the soil since ancient times. They improve the soil texture and add nitrogen compounds to the soil. Chemical fertiliser, also

11

It all depends on ...

Interdependence – other examples

containing nitrogen, increases plant growth and crop production. Fertiliser production uses a lot of energy. The global production of nitrogen fertiliser is around 160 million tonnes per year.

Active Learning

Activity

1. Using library and Internet resources find out more about chemicals inside cells that contain nitrogen.

2. Design an investigation to demonstrate the effect of nitrate concentration on plant growth. Consider the following points:

   a) Which plant variety will you use?

   b) How will you vary the nitrate concentration, for example, you may use ready-made fertiliser pellets or nitrate solutions?

   c) How will you design a control?

   d) What measurements will you make in order to determine the effect on 'plant growth'?

   e) What do your results tell you about the **optimum** design for a nitrate-based fertiliser?

Eutrophication (you-trow-fick-ah-shun)

Excess nitrates drain from fields into streams and rivers. The nitrates then promote the growth of water plants such as single-celled algae. A high concentration of nutrients in aquatic habitats is known as **eutrophication**. Such nutrient enrichment can lead to the formation of '**algal blooms**' which can affect other water organisms.

An algal bloom

The increased growth of surface algae stops the light from passing through the surface of the water and reaching plants which grow beneath the surface. Their growth is inhibited as they are unable to photosynthesise and they die. When the surface algae die, they sink to the bottom of the water. The increase in decomposition as a result of the greater volume of plants reduces the oxygen concentration of the water which can affect the fish living there.

Harmful algal blooms also happen in the ocean but scientists do not yet fully understand why they appear. The harmful algae release chemicals that are toxic

It all depends on ...

to other organisms. Each year, regions around the Scottish coastline are monitored for algal growth and levels of toxins in the water. If humans eat shellfish, such as scallops, oysters or mussels, where this toxin has built up, they can become very ill and possibly die. The Scottish Government has used its protective public health powers to regulate the harvesting of shellfish in Scottish waters.

An algal bloom as seen from a satellite

Active Learning

Activity

1 Construct a flow chart to summarise the causes and effects of eutrophication in a lake.

2 Research the term 'amnesic shellfish poisoning' and find out how this has affected the shellfish industry in Scotland in recent years.

Interdependence – symbiosis (sim-by-oh-sis)

Living things all depend on each other. Some depend on each other so closely that they live together in a partnership called '**symbiosis**'.

The micro-organisms in a cow's stomach help it to digest grass.

Cows are able to digest grass and plant fibre because billions of symbiotic micro-organisms do it for them. Bacteria and **protists** in particular fill one of their stomachs (cows have four stomachs!). These organisms benefit by getting somewhere to live and the cow benefits by receiving the products of digested grass. These symbiotic organisms also make protein and vitamins for the cow.

Some **parasites** can live *on* our bodies, such as fleas and body lice, while others live *inside* our bodies, including roundworms, tapeworms and flatworms.

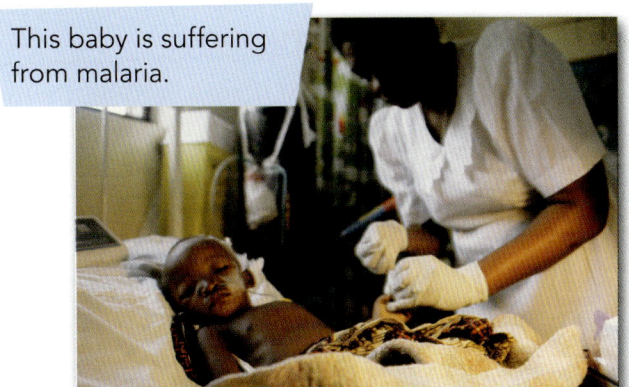

This baby is suffering from malaria.

Malaria is caused by a parasite which enters the blood from the bite of the female *Anopheles* (An-off-oh-lees) mosquito. (The males do not feed on blood.) Although we know a lot about the parasite

13

It all depends on …

Interdependence – other examples

and have developed drugs to prevent infection and treat the disease, each year up to 500 million people are infected with malaria, leading to as many as 2.7 million deaths.

The reasons why malaria is such a problem are complex and are due to both the biology of the parasite and to society.

The mosquito is found in warmer countries, which also tend to be the poorer ones. Another problem is resistance to the drugs most commonly used for treatment. More effective medicines are available but can be extremely expensive.

Over 90% of new cases are in sub-Saharan Africa. Poor people are affected more by malaria because they lack information about health services and preventative measures. Their poor living conditions also contribute – they may live in badly drained areas, close to swamps or in poorly constructed buildings with no protection from insects.

Affordable solutions to the malaria problem include rapid diagnosis and treatment of infected people, the use of mosquito nets impregnated with insecticide, the spraying of insecticides inside homes and the draining of stagnant water where mosquitoes breed.

Adaptation

The theory of evolution by natural selection was first proposed by Charles Darwin in his 1859 book *On the Origin of Species by Means of Natural Selection*. The theory of evolution is widely accepted by scientists since it is supported by lots of evidence.

Darwin's theory suggests that each species is adapted to its own way of life and its particular environment.

Behavioural adaptation

Some animals have adapted their behaviour in order to increase their chances of survival. Starlings, for example, have adapted to move in huge flocks during the winter months. This helps to protect individuals from their predators. Other birds migrate to favourable environments during the spring and autumn.

'Nothing in biology makes sense except in the light of evolution.'

Dobzhansky, *American Biology Teacher*, 1973

'Today the theory of evolution is about as much open to doubt as the theory that the Earth goes around the Sun.'

Richard Dawkins, *The Selfish Gene*, 1976

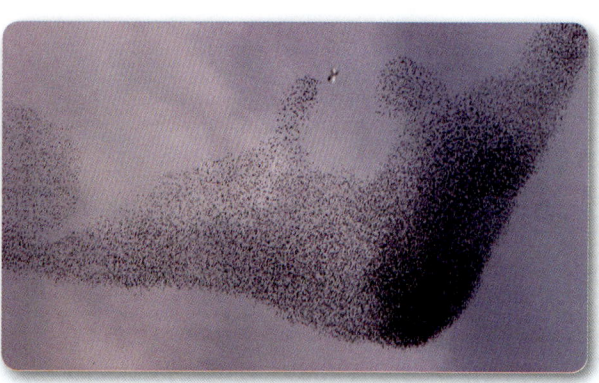

Starlings move in huge flocks to protect themselves from predators.

It all depends on …

Adaptation

Colour adaptation

The colours of living things are often adapted to their environment. Flowers are brightly coloured to attract insects and leaves are coloured green to trap sunlight. Coloured leaves trap light energy from different parts of the spectrum. Animals are often camouflaged to protect them from predators or brightly coloured to warn competitors.

Physiological adaptation

The physiology of an animal shows how it is adapted to its environment. While we sweat to lose heat, dogs pant – they only have sweat glands on their feet. Elephants have large ears and this helps them lose heat. Other animals, such as polar bears, are adapted to slow down their metabolism almost completely during the winter in a process known as **hibernation**. In Britain only hedgehogs, dormice and bats hibernate. Hibernating animals' heart rate, breathing rate, digestion and other vital processes slow down almost to zero during the winter when their food is in short supply.

Reproductive adaptation

Adaptations can influence any part of the reproductive cycle of living things. Male birds' behaviour is often adapted to attract females with which to mate, for example a male peacock fanning its tail, a blackbird singing on your roof or a robin's aggressive display to other males. Reproductive processes – mating in animals and flowering in plants – can be adapted to respond to favourable environmental conditions and respond to seasonal changes. Although roe deer mate in August, they have an unusual adaptation whereby the fertilised egg does not implant and start to develop until December. This delayed implantation ensures that the fawns are born at the correct time in the spring.

Cuttlefish are adapted to change their appearance quickly and match their background.

These bats are hibernating.

Roe deer

15

It all depends on ...

Adaptation

Structural adaptation

Many animals, birds in particular, show structural adaptations to their environment. The beak or bill of a bird can be any number of shapes to help it to access its food supply more easily.

The curlew's bill is adapted to pick worms from estuarine mud and the robin's beak is adapted to preying on worms, seeds, fruits and insects.

Population growth

👍 The **populations** of living things are constantly changing.

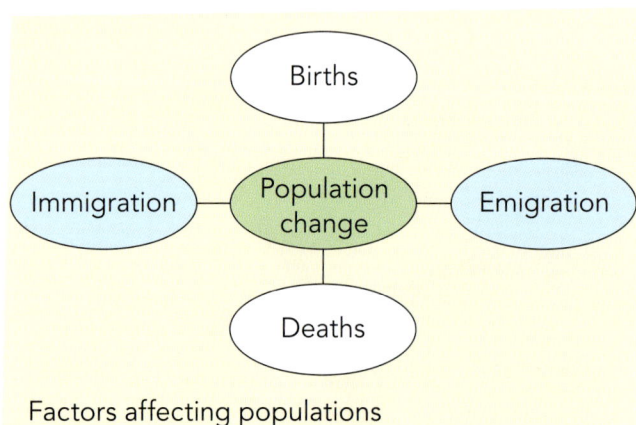

Factors affecting populations

All living things die. Death is an essential aspect of life. Mayfly young live the great majority of their lives as nymphs in freshwater. The adults emerge from the water during a short period. Each one survives a short time, from a few minutes to 2 days, mates and then dies.

Fishing flies are used to lure trout. They often mimic mayflies.

Births and new growth are often seasonal. For example, lambs are born in the late winter but by the time they are weaned from their mother's milk, new grass has grown for them to eat.

16

It all depends on ...

Population growth

Age, disease, food availability and predation all contribute to death rates.

Immigration, entering a population, and **emigration**, leaving a population, both influence the size of a population. Winter populations of geese and summer populations of swallows are examples of seasonal migration into and out of Scotland.

Active Learning

Activity

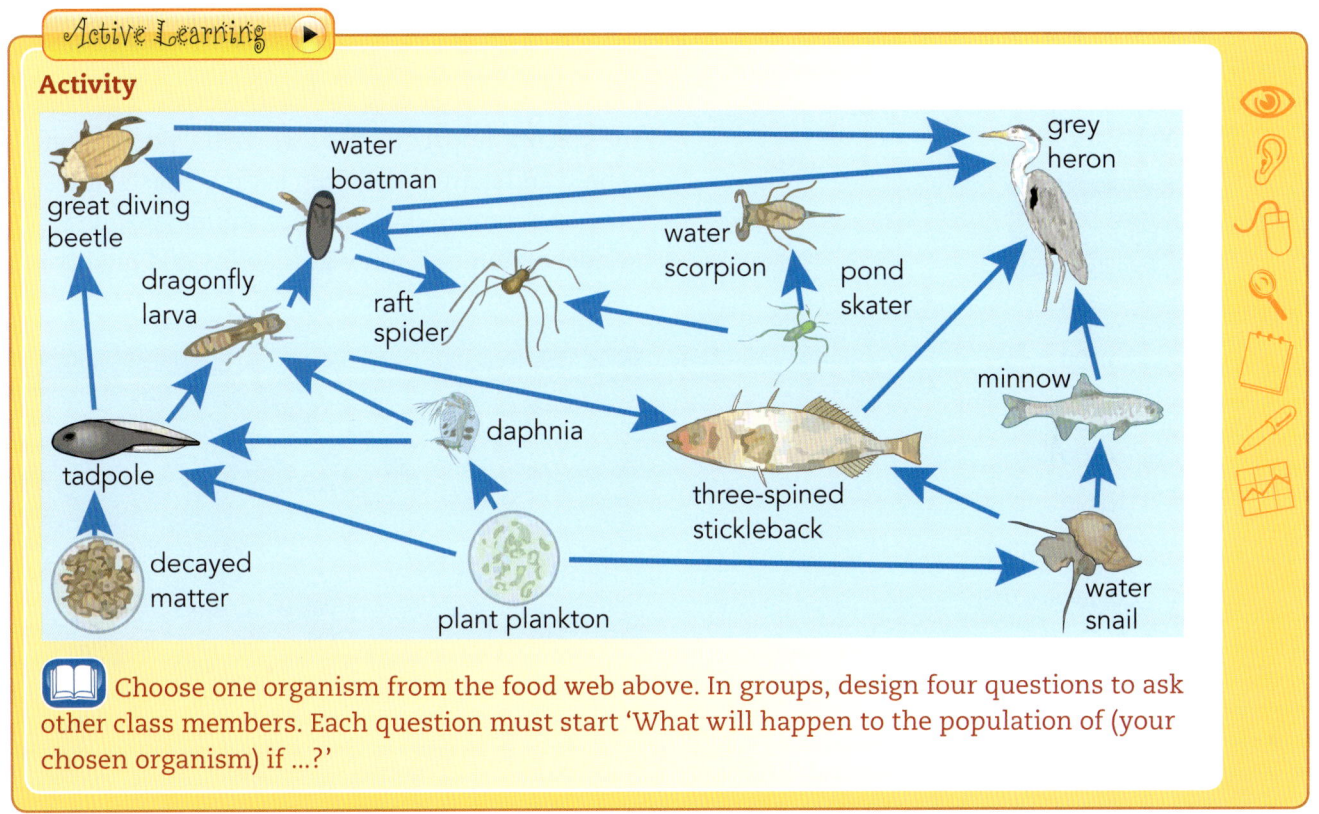

Choose one organism from the food web above. In groups, design four questions to ask other class members. Each question must start 'What will happen to the population of (your chosen organism) if ...?'

Human population

The number of people on the Earth is growing at an alarming rate. More people are being born than are dying.

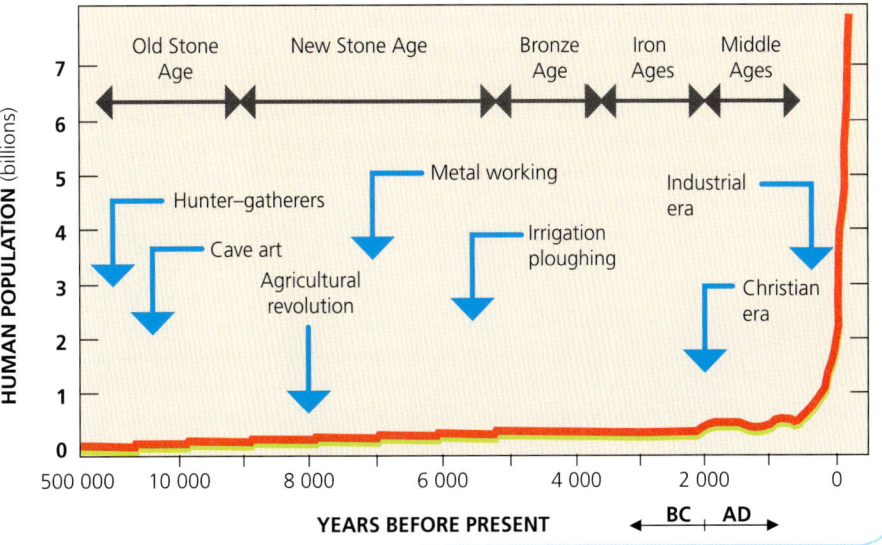

Human population growth during the past half a million years

It all depends on ...

Human population

The graph shows that the human population slowly increased during history. Life expectancy has been rising steadily since the start of the industrial era as a result of scientific, medical and nutritional advances. During the past 200 years the graph has become 'J-shaped' indicating that the rate of population growth is accelerating rapidly. Human population growth is the biggest issue facing humanity today.

Year	Estimated population (millions)
1900	600
1925	1 300
1950	2 400
1975	4 100
2000	6 100
2025	7 800
2050	8 700

Active Learning

Activity

1. 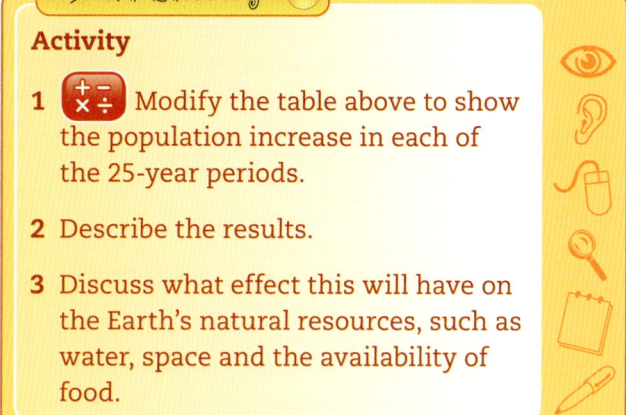 Modify the table above to show the population increase in each of the 25-year periods.
2. Describe the results.
3. Discuss what effect this will have on the Earth's natural resources, such as water, space and the availability of food.

Natural hazards affect all populations – and humans are included. Dramatic geographical, geological and biological events affect populations of all organisms. Floods, cyclones, droughts, fires and heat waves are related to climate change, deforestation and the world's weather systems. Earthquakes, volcanoes and tsunamis are all the result of movements in the Earth's crust. They have the greatest impact in areas where the population is high and natural defences, such as coastal forest, have been removed. Epidemics, animal plagues, accidental injuries, water availability and quality, and war also affect populations.

Huge catastrophes will take place in the future. We know that asteroid collisions and supervolcanoes have taken place in the past. We also know that they are going to happen again.

The risk and impact of natural disasters is increasing, largely as a response to the growing human population. Natural disasters influence human populations and all of biodiversity and this is leading to a reduction in the variety of living things that are surviving on the planet.

It all depends on ...

An orang-utan orphan

The orang-utan's habitat is being rapidly replaced by palm plantations to satisfy the world's growing need for palm oil. Ninety per cent of the population of orang-utans has been lost in the last 100 years. The WWF warns that orang-utans might become extinct within 20 years if preventative action is not taken.

QUESTIONS

1. List the advantages that pollinating insects gain in their partnership with flowers.
2. Construct a flow chart to show the main stages of the flowering plant life cycle.
3. Complete the three sentences that summarise population change.

   When the birth rate is { greater than / the same as / less than } the death rate the population will { stay the same / increase / decrease }.

4. 'Human population growth is the biggest issue facing humanity today.' Find evidence to support this statement.
5. Make a table that summarises the natural hazards mentioned in the chapter and list their effects.
6. 📖 Carry out some research on one of the following topics: animal migration, supervolcanoes, asteroid collisions or endangered species. Write up your findings in a short report.

GLOSSARY

Adaptation Organism design to enable survival in its surroundings

Aerobic respiration Energy release involving oxygen

Biotic Related to living things

Parasite Organism that lives on another one and causes harm

Population All the members of a species living in a particular area

Protist Single-celled organism

19

PLANET EARTH
Biodiversity and Interdependence

Plant growth and reproduction

Level 3 — What came before?

 SCN 3-02a

I have collaborated on investigations into the process of photosynthesis and I can demonstrate my understanding of why plants are vital to sustaining life on Earth.

 SCN 3-14a

I understand the processes of fertilisation and embryonic development and can discuss possible risks to the embryo.

Level 4 — What is this chapter about?

 SCN 4-02a

I have propagated and grown plants using a variety of different methods. I can compare these methods and develop my understanding of their commercial use.

 SCN 4-14b

Through evaluation of a range of data, I can compare sexual and asexual reproduction and explain their importance for survival of species.

Plant growth and reproduction

Plant propagation

Propagation increases the numbers of living things. Plants can be propagated from seeds or from their tissues.

Flowers are reproductive organs. Flowers usually contain male and female parts (occasionally these are found on different plants as complete male or female flowers). The male part is called the **stamen** and produces pollen which contains the male sex cell. The female part is called the **carpel** and this makes the ovule (the female sex cell).

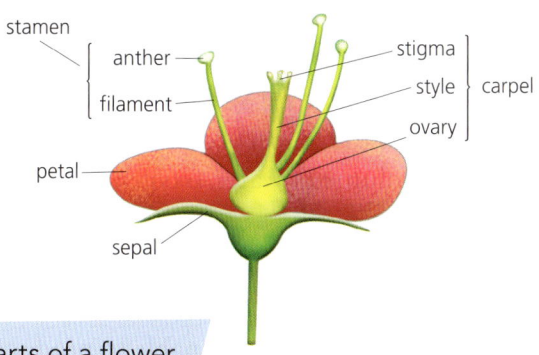

The parts of a flower

Pollen is transferred from the stamen of one flower to the stigma of another mainly by wind or insects. A pollen tube then grows through the style to the ovary and carries the male sex cell to the female sex cell where fertilisation takes place. The fertilised ovum will now form a seed.

Plant propagation with seeds

Plant numbers can be increased by sowing seeds. Seeds are the product of sexual reproduction in flowering plants and contain genetic information that came from two parent plants. This means that seeds are genetically different from each other. The development of a seed is controlled by the genetic information that is found in the nucleus of the cells in the embryo.

Farmers sow and harvest vast numbers of seeds around the world each year. Major crops – cereals, vegetables and fruits – are grown from seeds to provide food, fuel and raw materials. Seeds exist in an enormous range of sizes and shapes. Peanuts and sunflower seeds are popular snacks.

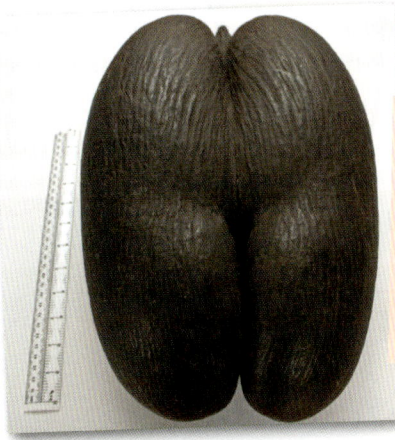

The world's largest seed comes from the Coco de Mer or double coconut and can weigh as much as 20 kg.

The smallest seeds are produced by orchids. These seeds are so small that they cannot be seen without a microscope. One seed can weigh as little as 0.8 micrograms.

Active Learning

Activity

Research structures that flowering plants produce in order to disperse their seeds.

PLANET EARTH
Biodiversity and Interdependence

Investigating aerobic respiration

Level 3 — What came before?

 SCN 3-12a
I have explored the structure and function of organs and organ systems and can relate this to the basic biological processes required to sustain life.

 SCN 3-13a
Using a microscope, I have developed my understanding of the structure and variety of cells and of their functions.

Level 4 — What is this chapter about?

 SCN 4-02b
I can contribute to the design of an investigation to show the effects of different factors on the rate of aerobic respiration and explain my findings.

Investigating aerobic respiration

Living things are effective energy converters. Remember that stored energy provides the capacity to do work and that living things work to produce heat, movement, light and other forms of energy. **Respiration** is the process that takes place inside organisms to release chemical energy and enable the energy conversions. Respiration occurs in cells with or without oxygen.

Respiration

Respiration in the absence of oxygen

Active Learning

Activity

Carry out the following experiment. You will need a partner to write down the results of the investigation and a bench clock for timing. With your hand by your side, make a clicking sound by flicking your thumb and forefinger together for 2 minutes.

Your partner should record the results in a table with three columns, as shown below:

Time (seconds)	Number of clicks	Loudness
10		
20		
30		

Repeat the experiment two more times, once with your arm extended horizontally and then finally with your hand above your head.

 Write a short report on each experimental trial. Think about two areas:

- What your results table shows you (graphs and charts can help).
- How you felt following the exercises.

Explanation

 Exercise places demands on your circulatory and respiratory systems since high levels of oxygen are needed. Blood carries oxygen to the muscles. It also

29

Investigating aerobic respiration

Respiration

transports dissolved food. Plenty of food is also stored in muscle cells. During light exercise the muscles receive sufficient oxygen to release energy for the activity. Heavy exercise relies on high levels of oxygen which the circulatory system is not always able to supply.

Muscle fatigue happens during oxygen shortage but the cells are still able to release small quantities of energy by **anaerobic** respiration. Anaerobic respiration leads to the production of **lactic acid** in the muscle cells. At this point, the activity should be stopped as muscle fatigue and pain develop.

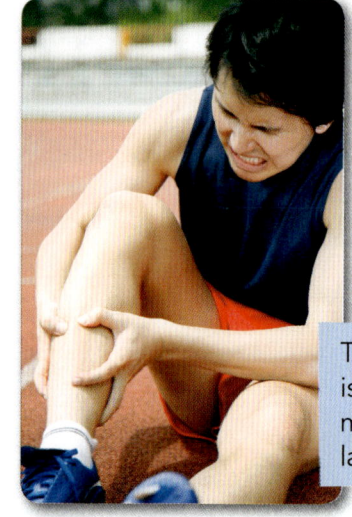

This marathon runner is experiencing muscle fatigue from lactic acid build-up.

All living things are energy changers. Anaerobic respiration in plants results in the production of ethanol, an alcohol, instead of lactic acid. The alcohol produced by yeast, a kind of fungus, is of particular economic importance in the brewing industry. In the baking industry the carbon dioxide produced by yeast causes dough to develop a spongy texture.

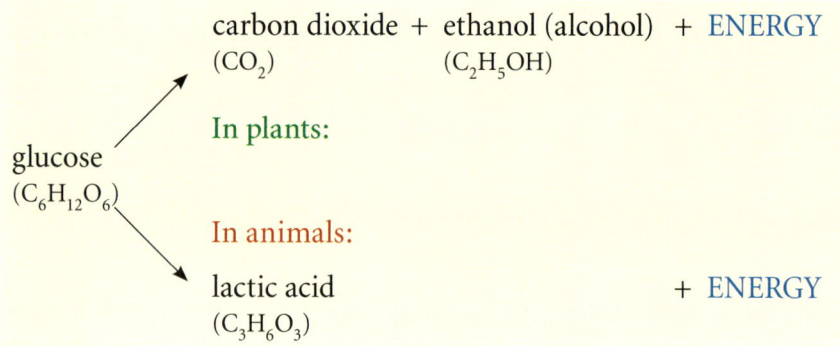

Cellular respiration and energy

Cells need energy. The process of cellular respiration takes place inside cells and releases energy from digested food. **Aerobic** respiration takes place in the presence of oxygen which is absorbed into the blood in the lungs. (You might have heard about 'aerobic exercise' which involves hard work and leads to increased breathing and circulation rates.)

Aerobic respiration summary

The rate of the respiration is influenced by the availability of the reactants. In the example of the fatigued muscle, insufficient oxygen is available to allow the muscles to respire aerobically, thus slowing the respiration. Oxygen is therefore

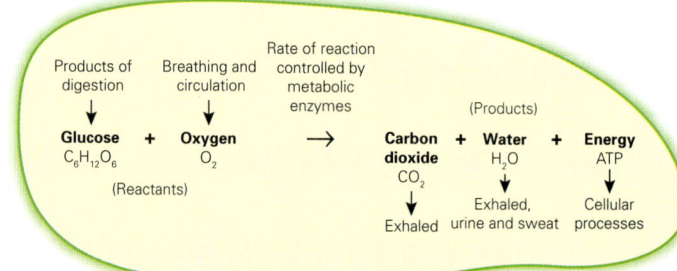

Investigating aerobic respiration

said to be the **limiting factor**. If sufficient levels of glucose and oxygen are available, then the rate of the reaction may be limited by temperature. Rates of reaction slow as temperatures reduce. The temperatures at which chemical reactions function at their highest level are termed the **optimum** (plural: optimums or optima).

Active Learning

Activity

A scientist recorded the core temperatures for a lizard and a mammal of similar size and varied the temperature of the environment. The results are shown on the following graph.

Write a report on the experiment that describes the results.

Identify which of the animals (A or B) is the mammal and which is the lizard.

List the conditions that you would include to ensure the animals did not suffer during the experiment.

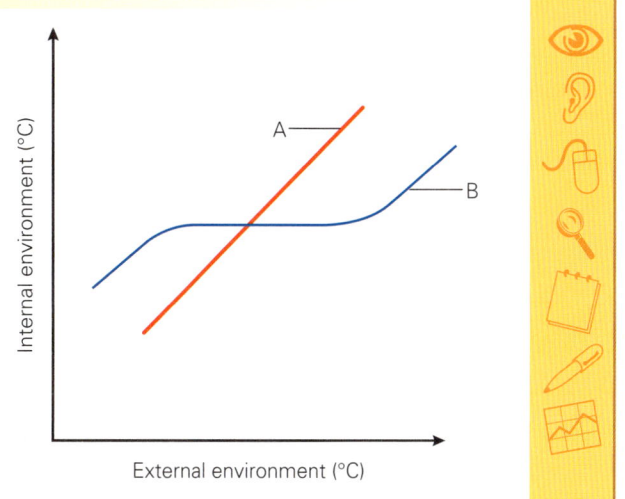

Active Learning

Activity

Use a carbon dioxide sensor and an oxygen sensor to measure and monitor the concentration of the gases in air surrounding germinating peas. The gas sensors can be connected to a computer which can monitor, record and display changes in gas concentration over periods of time.

Look at the results over different time periods.

Discuss the variables that could be investigated using this approach.

Investigating aerobic respiration

Respiration

Active Learning

Activity

Investigate the rate of aerobic respiration using the following apparatus.

Yeast releases carbon dioxide gas when it respires. The aim of this investigation is to use the number of bubbles of gas coming out of the apparatus as a measure of the rate of respiration. Colour change in the bicarbonate indicator (from red to orange to yellow) is an additional measure of respiration.

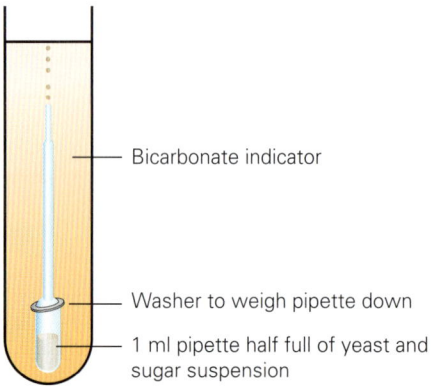

It is possible to use this apparatus to investigate the following variables. Can you think of any other variables that might affect the rate of respiration?

- **Temperature** – by placing the apparatus in a water bath or ice bath.
- **Raw materials** – by adding different concentrations of sucrose, glucose and distilled water.
- **Yeast** – the effect of different varieties and different concentrations.

Factors which influence the aerobic respiration rate

An organism's rate of aerobic respiration depends on its level of activity and environmental factors such as temperature, food availability and the seasonal fluctuations in day length. Body size and stage of development also affect respiration rates, as does an organism's behaviour.

Active Learning

Activity

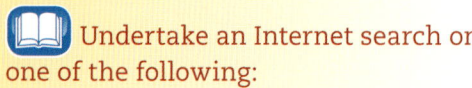 Undertake an Internet search on one of the following:

- Examples of humans surviving being submerged for a time in water under ice.
- Basal metabolic rate (BMR) and the factors affecting it.
- The difference between breathing and respiration.
- How and why the body is cooled during open heart surgery.

Present your research to the class.

Investigating aerobic respiration

> **Active Learning**
>
> **Activity**
>
> A simple respirometer can be used to measure the rate of respiration of an animal.
>
>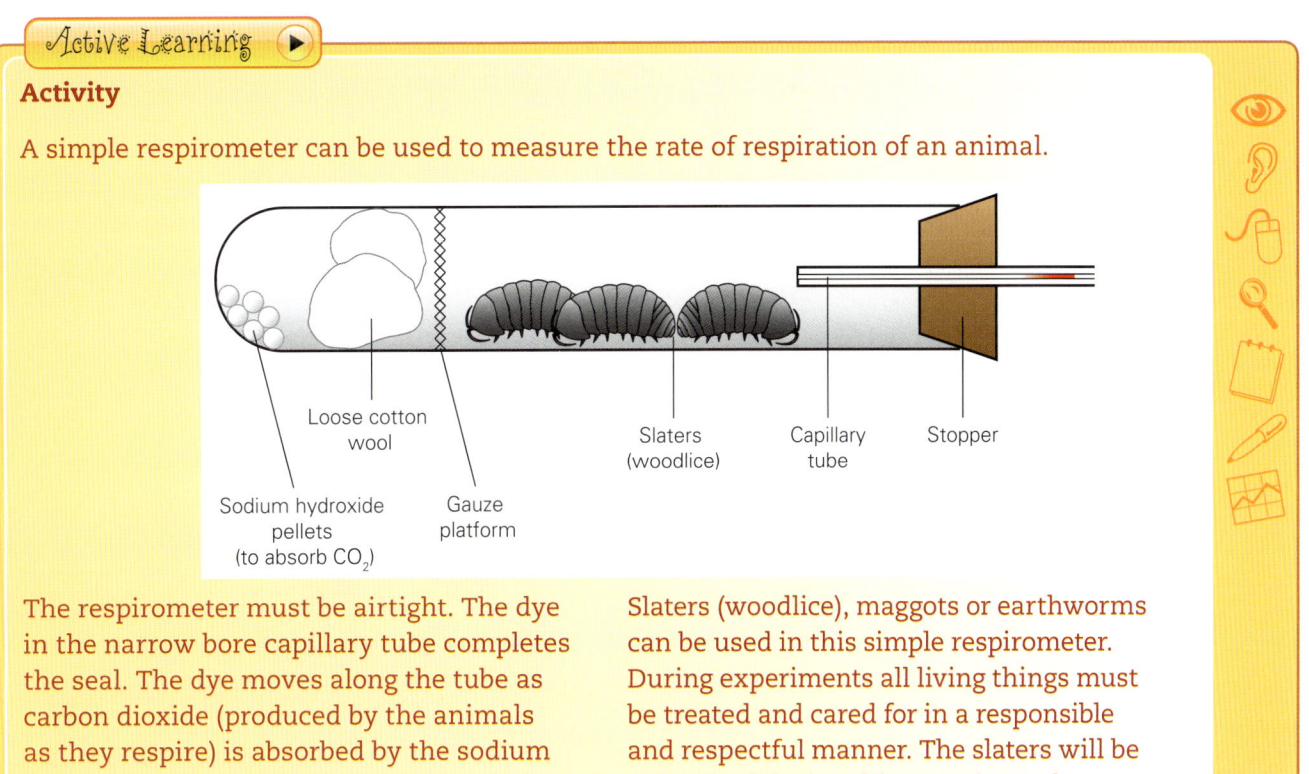
>
> Loose cotton wool
> Slaters (woodlice)
> Capillary tube
> Stopper
> Sodium hydroxide pellets (to absorb CO$_2$)
> Gauze platform
>
> The respirometer must be airtight. The dye in the narrow bore capillary tube completes the seal. The dye moves along the tube as carbon dioxide (produced by the animals as they respire) is absorbed by the sodium hydroxide. Measuring the distance moved over time can be used as a measure of the rate of respiration.
>
> Slaters (woodlice), maggots or earthworms can be used in this simple respirometer. During experiments all living things must be treated and cared for in a responsible and respectful manner. The slaters will be unharmed during this experiment because the cotton wool barrier will protect them from the toxic effects of the sodium hydroxide pellets. Following the experiment the organisms should be returned to their habitat.

Respiration and photosynthesis in plants

Respiration is the biochemical process that releases energy in living things. It is carried out by all living things. Respiration releases carbon dioxide which is one of the raw materials (substrates) for photosynthesis.

Photosynthesis is the biochemical process that traps the Sun's energy and uses it to make all the biochemical materials in the plant as well as providing the base for food chains. Photosynthesis uses carbon dioxide which is a product of respiration.

This circulation of carbon between the atmosphere and food chains is the basis of the carbon cycle.

Investigating aerobic respiration

Respiration and photosynthesis in plants

As plants respire all the time, in the light and in the dark, they produce carbon dioxide all the time. This carbon dioxide is used as a substrate for photosynthesis; when the light intensity is sufficiently high it is converted into glucose.

Active Learning

Activity

Set up the apparatus as shown and leave illuminated until your next science lesson. Write a report on the experiment and explain the results in terms of photosynthesis and respiration.

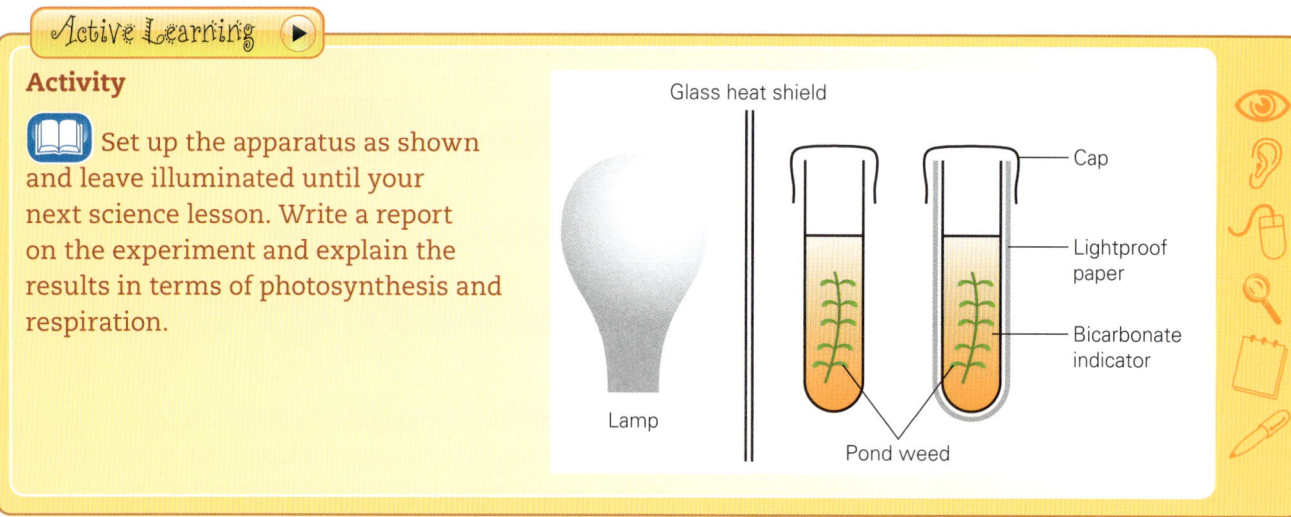

QUESTIONS

1. Find examples of each of the following energy conversion which happen in nature:
   a) Chemical → Light
   b) Light → Chemical
   c) Chemical → Electrical
   d) Chemical → Heat

2. Find out more about where respiration takes place inside living cells.

3. Explain why:
   a) The rate of respiration in a plant may increase during the day and decline again at night.
   b) The levels of oxygen and carbon dioxide in an enclosed, transparent container containing a plant sitting at a window will change during a 24-hour period.

4. Explain why it is an advantage for a human to develop muscle pain following periods of anaerobic respiration.

5. Look at the figure on page 30 that summarises the biochemical changes involved in aerobic respiration. Write a few sentences to explain these changes, for example 'Glucose is produced by the digestion of food'.

GLOSSARY

Aerobic With oxygen

Anaerobic Without oxygen

Optimum Ideal conditions

Respiration Biochemical process that releases energy from chemical sources

PLANET EARTH
Energy Sources and Sustainability

Saving the planet

Level 3 — What came before?

● SCN 3-04a
I can use my knowledge of the different ways in which heat is transferred between hot and cold objects and the thermal conductivity of materials to improve energy efficiency in buildings or other systems.

● SCN 3-04b
By investigating renewable energy sources and taking part in practical activities to harness them, I can discuss their benefits and potential problems.

● SCN 3-03a
Through investigations and based on experimental evidence, I can explain the use of different types of chemicals in agriculture and their alternatives and can evaluate their potential impact on the world's food production.

Level 4 — What is this chapter about?

● SCN 4-04a
By contributing to an investigation on different ways of meeting society's energy needs, I can express an informed view on the risks and benefits of different energy sources, including those produced from plants.

● SCN 4-04b
Through investigation, I can explain the formation and use of fossil fuels and contribute to discussions on the responsible use and conservation of finite resources.

● SCN 4-18a
I can monitor the environment by collecting and analysing samples. I can interpret the results to inform others about levels of pollution and express a considered opinion on how science can help to protect our environment.

35

Saving the planet

What an atmosphere!

The Earth's atmosphere refers to the thin layer of gases that surrounds the surface of the planet. It is made up of a mixture of gases, mainly nitrogen, oxygen, argon and carbon dioxide along with traces of others.

The proportions of the different gases remain fairly constant: about 78% nitrogen, 21% oxygen, 0.1% argon and 0.04% carbon dioxide. This is achieved by the chemical reactions involved in nutrient cycles such as the nitrogen cycle and the carbon cycle. However, human activity influences these natural cycles and can lead to disturbance of the balance of atmospheric gases.

Active Learning

Activity

Using coloured beads to represent the molecules of different gases in the air, make a model showing the relative proportions of the gases in a glass jar or beaker.

Combustion

The development of the steam engine in the late eighteenth century led to the Industrial Revolution. From that time onwards the burning of fossil fuels has increased to provide energy for agriculture, industry and transport.

Fossil fuels like coal, oil, peat and natural gas are energy-rich fuels. They contain stores of chemical energy that can be burned in the presence of oxygen to release large quantities of heat energy. While the use of fossil fuels has improved standards of living vastly since the early nineteenth century, there have been some disadvantages to their continued use. When fossil fuels are burned, they release carbon dioxide into the atmosphere. This has led to increased carbon dioxide levels within the atmosphere. This, along with the production of other carbon-containing gases such

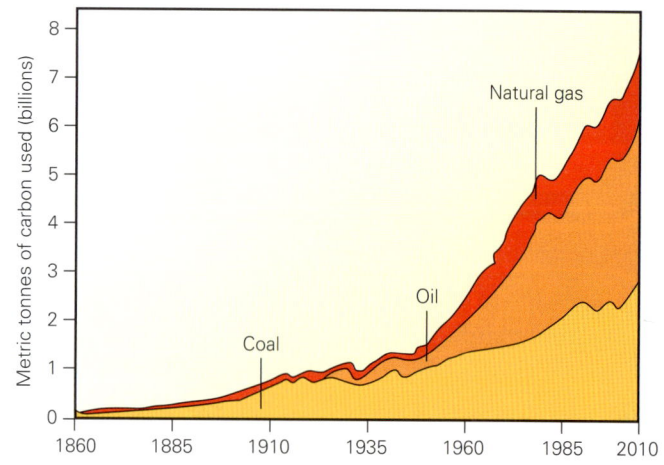

Growth in fossil fuel consumption

Saving the planet

Combustion

as methane, has added to a problem described as the **Greenhouse Effect**, whereby the build-up of particular gases in the air traps heat energy near to the surface of the Earth, leading to **global warming**.

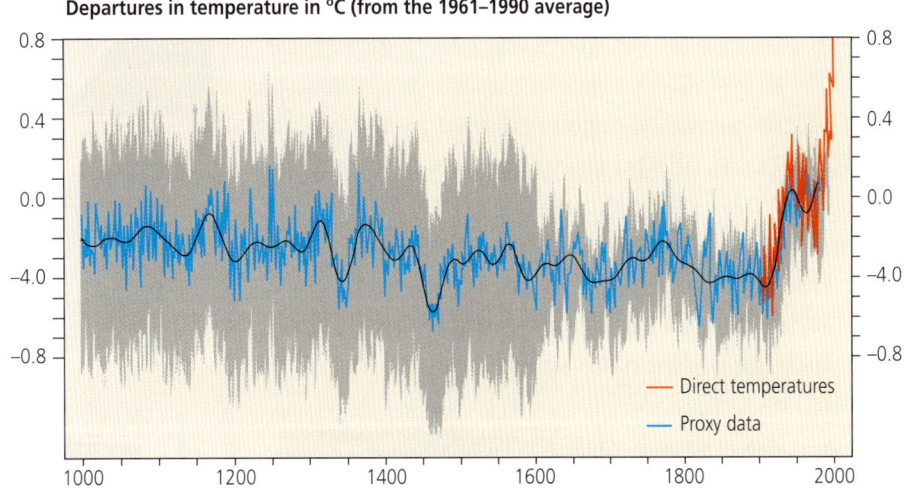

Variations in the Earth's surface temperature over the last 1000 years for the Northern Hemisphere (source: IPCC Climate Change 2002 Synthesis Report).

While politicians and scientists debate the possible outcomes of global warming, this graph shows that average temperatures have increased during the past 1000 years. The temperature has increased most dramatically since the start of the Industrial Revolution and matches the data pattern for increased fuel use.

Fossil fuels often contain compounds of sulphur or nitrogen. When the fuels are burned, oxides of these chemicals can be released into the atmosphere. These gases contribute to air pollution and acid rain which has many detrimental effects on living things and their habitats. The soot produced when fossil fuels are burned also damages the environment.

Active Learning

Activity

Find out more about a named air pollutant. What is the main source(s) of the pollutant? How can it be detected? What steps can be taken to reduce/eliminate it from the air?

Long-term use of fossil fuels

Fossil fuels and the products derived from them are hugely important to our lives. Think of any 24-hour period and you will have relied on fossil fuels to keep you warm, help you see more clearly, power machinery and get around. The problem is, these fuels took millions of years to form, but they are burned in a matter of hours. This makes fossil fuels a finite resource. They are effectively non-renewable as we simply cannot replace them as quickly as they are being used up. Non-replacement, as well as the problems relating to pollution, has meant that alternative renewable sources of energy have had to be found.

Saving the planet

Long-term use of fossil fuels

Fossil fuels: a burning issue

Industry and our homes are full of machines that consume energy. Modern transport allows us to travel more often and much further than our ancestors.

Most of this energy has been provided by the burning of coal, oil and gas to generate electricity. Fossil fuels have provided us with relatively cheap and easy-to-use sources of energy. But they do release polluting gases into the atmosphere. Habitat destruction also results from mining for fossil fuels. In addition, oil spills harm ocean wildlife.

All these devices consume energy.

The devastating effects of an oil spill.

A major use of coal throughout the world is the generation of electricity in power stations. It has been estimated that 41% of the world's electricity is produced by burning coal. In some countries the figure is much higher. In Australia, for example, almost 80% of the electricity is produced in coal-burning power stations.

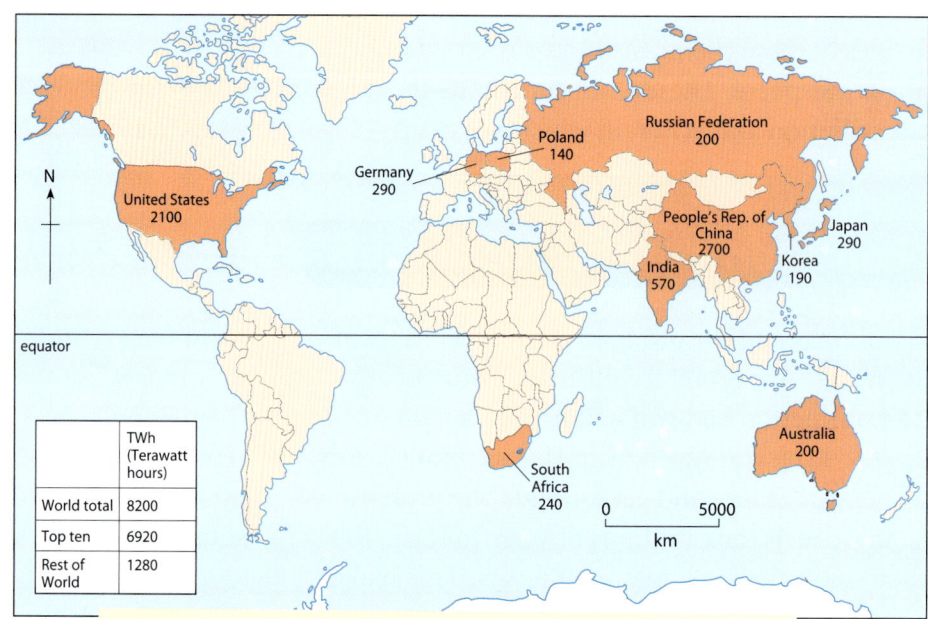

	TWh (Terawatt hours)
World total	8200
Top ten	6920
Rest of World	1280

Terawatt-hours of electricity produced by the burning of coal by country (source: OECD).

Saving the planet

Clearly the world is still very dependent on coal as an energy source but things are changing. The electricity industry is trying to burn less coal by developing more efficient power stations. It is also trying to become cleaner and reduce the amount of harmful pollutants it produces. It has already developed technology that reduces the gases that cause acid rain but the big challenge is to reduce carbon dioxide emissions. Scientists are trying to develop technologies that can trap the polluting carbon dioxide and store it in order to prevent it entering the atmosphere and causing climate change. Already there are some pilot projects trying to carry out carbon capture and storage (CCS). At the Longannet power station in Scotland, some of the carbon dioxide produced is being trapped using chemicals and eventually it will be stored under the sea. In another project, the Drax power station in England has reduced carbon dioxide output by 12% by using renewable plant material and coal to produce electricity.

Active Learning

Activity

1 Make a table illustrating the advantages and disadvantages of using fossil fuels as energy sources.

2 Use the Internet and library resources to research how long the planet's reserves of coal are likely to last.

3 Write a short story to describe how you think the world is likely to change in the future. How will electricity be produced? What sources of energy will be used? How will transport change?

Biorenewables

It is estimated that by 2050 the world will require double the energy that is currently used while aiming to reduce carbon emissions by 50%. As the population of our planet continues to rise, supplies of fossil fuels cannot keep pace.

Renewable sources of energy may struggle to fill the gap between supply and demand and nuclear generation of electricity, with its own environmental challenges, may be required to meet our energy demands. Future oil supplies and prices are unpredictable. Global climate change will influence nations' energy choices and as a result there is a great need to develop alternative, affordable, effective sources of renewable energy to sustain our increasing requirements.

Renewable energy sources produce electricity or heat without depleting our planet's limited resources. **Biorenewables**, also known as

Edinburgh by night

biomass, are produced by living things. They include agricultural crops and wood produced by photosynthesis, as well as animal waste.

Biorenewables may generate heat from the direct use of the flammable materials as a fuel or they may be converted into liquids and gases.

Saving the planet

Biorenewables

Ethanol, a biofuel, is manufactured by converting the cellulose or starch in the biomass into sugar which is then fermented into alcohol (ethanol). Ethanol can be used to power cars. It is produced by fermenting the sugar or starch in sugar cane, sugar beet, wheat, maize or wood pulp into ethanol.

Biodiesel is produced by mixing alcohol with oils that have been extracted from plants such as rape seed, soybean or from waste vegetable oils.

A rape seed field

Conflict may arise in the future between food and fuel production on finite land resources.

Biogas is produced from decomposing animal or plant waste. It has a high methane content.

Landfill biogas burns to generate electricity.

Anaerobic digestion is carried out by bacteria. It is used to break down sewage, food waste and other organic materials to produce methane gas. The solid remains can be spread on fields as fertiliser.

Crops grown as fuels include food crops such as sugar cane and corn, grasses and rapidly growing trees.

Syngas

Biomass can be heated at relatively high temperatures in the absence of oxygen to produce a gaseous or liquid fuel. The gas mixture is called '**syngas**' – short for synthetic gas. Syngas is a mixture of methane and carbon monoxide and has lower energy values than natural gas.

Syngas

Scientists and engineers are exploring the use of seaweed, marine algae, as a source of biofuel as they would not require farmland or fresh water.

The largest source of biomass in the UK (about 40% of the total) is waste wood. Production could be extended to developing areas of woodland that are currently unmanaged. Wood fuel is a renewable source of energy that 'grows on trees'! It is a sustainable, low carbon source of energy that

A soft wood forest

40 Biorenewables

Saving the planet

can be produced from rapidly growing soft wood timber of low commercial value in a managed woodland where felled trees are replaced by young trees.

> **Active Learning**
>
> **Activity**
>
> Find out more about the five basic categories of biomass: burning wood, burning rubbish, alcohol fuels, crops and landfill gas.

> **Active Learning**
>
> **Activity**
>
> In groups develop a marketing strategy to encourage the use of wood as a fuel. Note that 12% of the UK is covered in woods and forests. **OR**
>
> Discuss what is meant by the forester's saying: 'The woodland that pays is the woodland that stays.' **OR**
>
> The efficiency of wood-burning stoves is always being improved. List the advantages and disadvantages of using wood as a fuel.

Biological indicators

The presence of bluebells in a wood tells us the time of the year – we know that they flower in spring.

They also suggest that the woodland is an ancient one. This can be confirmed by looking for other **indicator species**.

Experienced observers are able to tell a great deal about the conditions that exist in a particular habitat, such as moisture and pH. They are also able to make comparisons between different habitats and different times of the year.

Lichens and sulphur dioxide (SO$_2$)

Lichens consist of algae and fungi living together. They receive water directly from the atmosphere and so they are especially sensitive to atmospheric pollutants. Sulphur dioxide (SO$_2$) is released when fossil fuels are burned. It then forms an acid when it combines with rainwater.

Branching lichens like this one are not found in areas with high SO$_2$ pollution.

Bluebells

Lichen

41

Saving the planet

Biological indicators

Seasonal indicators

The science of **phenology** provides opportunities for everyone to collect and report significant data about seasonal events. Collected data demonstrates that in the UK, spring events are happening earlier and autumn is starting later and lasting longer. Scientists say that these observations demonstrate the reality of climate change.

Phenology is the study of the timing of recurring natural phenomena especially in relation to climate. Trees coming into leaf or the arrival of migratory birds are two examples.

'Become a recorder at nature's calendar'

www.naturescalendar.org.uk

Data collection

Climate change, a normal part of the Earth's evolution, is brought about by complex natural processes. Computer modelling suggests that global **mean** temperatures are rising due to the emissions of greenhouse gases.

Mechanical data collection is time consuming. It can include measuring soil temperatures with a thermometer, collecting water samples and carrying out laboratory analysis. In the UK, air quality is monitored automatically in more than 1500 locations. The advantages are that a large number of factors can be measured every hour, including gases such as sulphur dioxide, nitrogen dioxide and ozone, organic materials from burnt fuel and microscopic particles.

Air quality monitoring stations are found throughout the country.

These stations collect data and pass them on through the Internet.

Saving the planet

QUESTIONS

1. Explain why fossil fuels are called non-renewable.
2. State three examples of renewable sources of energy.
3. a) Write one terawatt in numbers.
   b) Calculate the total energy production from coal from the top ten countries shown on the world map.
   c) Express this sum as a percentage of the total world energy production from coal.
4. Name two sources of energy, other than coal, used in power stations.
5. Find out how much of the electricity generated in Scotland today comes from fossil-fuel-powered power stations.
6. Research the formation of three fossil fuels and produce a presentation that describes the differences in how they were formed and in their properties.
7. Find out more about the causes of and the possible solutions to global warming.
8. Explain this sentence as fully as possible in your own words: 'Conflict may arise in the future between food and fuel production on finite land resources.'

GLOSSARY

Biorenewables Fuel sources derived from living materials

Global warming Gradual increase in the Earth's temperature which is contributing to climate change

Greenhouse Effect The trapping of heat energy close to the Earth's surface due to build up of certain gases including carbon dioxide and methane

Mean A statistical term meaning the arithmetical average

Terawatt A million million watts

BIOLOGICAL SYSTEMS
Body Systems and Cells

5 Finding a perfect balance

Level 3 — What came before?

SCN 3-12a

I have explored the structure and function of organs and organ systems and can relate this to the basic biological processes required to sustain life.

Level 4 — What is this chapter about?

SCN 4-12a

I can explain how biological actions which take place in response to external and internal changes work to maintain stable body conditions.

Finding a perfect balance

Cells, tissues and organs will only **metabolise** correctly within a small range of conditions. They control their internal environment carefully, monitoring the pH and the concentration of nutrients, salts, waste and gases.

Central heating – a model of physiological control

Control centre – a programmer allows us to control the system: when the heating comes on, at what temperature etc.

Receptor – thermostats in rooms and on radiators detect the temperature around the house.

Effector – the boiler is turned on to raise the temperature to the desired level or turned off to let it fall. It is controlled by the programmer.

Physiological control relies on receptors informing the control centre and effectors returning conditions to the required level. **Receptors** are found in the sensory system and they monitor internal and external conditions. The **control centre** lies in the central nervous system and the brain. The **effectors** are found in the cells, tissues and organs.

Optimum

These three syllables make a BIG SCIENTIFIC WORD.

Optimum is a term used by scientists to describe the *conditions* at which the *maximum* response is found. Physiological systems set conditions at particular levels to ensure that they are kept within ranges that permit optimum responses in cells and the entire organism.

Optimum can refer to the conditions inside cells, entire organisms and the environment.

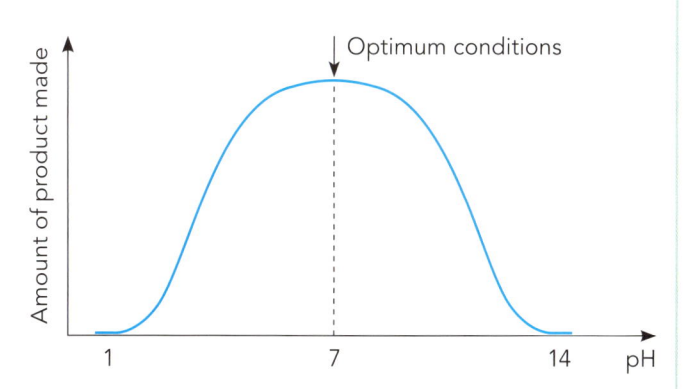

45

Finding a perfect balance

Case 1: Temperature control in humans

The control centre in the brain sets the body temperature at around 37 °C. Individuals' oral temperatures, taken under the tongue, can vary from 36.4 °C to 37.3 °C. The axillary (armpit) temperature normally varies from 35.9 °C to 36.7 °C. The exact temperature depends on which part of the body the measurement is being taken from. Body temperature also varies with age, level of activity and time of day.

The human body can maintain its temperature in any environmental conditions.

Active Learning

Activity

Your temperature can be taken with a variety of different thermometers. It can also be taken from a variety of places in your body. Accuracy is very important.

Discuss how and where you will take your temperature. Record it and insert it into a database of results for the whole class and the whole school.

A digital clinical thermometer

Find the following in the database:

- the lowest temperature
- the highest temperature
- the most common temperature
- the mean temperature.

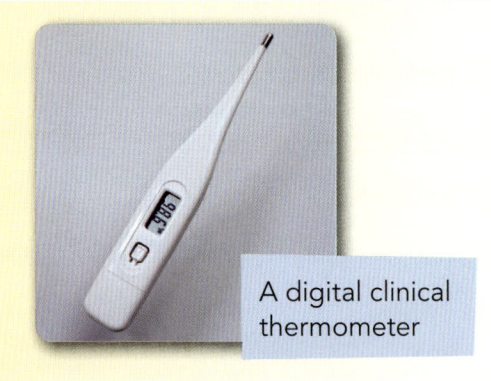

Class	Subject	Temperature (°C)
3.6	57	36.2
3.6	58	37.1
2.2	59	
2.2	60	
	61	
	62	
	63	
	64	

Finding a perfect balance

Heat gain effectors include those that bring about shivering, drawing blood away from the surface of the skin and causing body hair to stand up (leading to goose pimples).

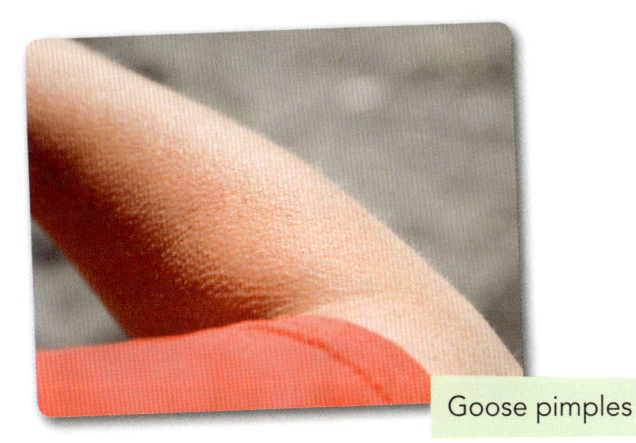

Goose pimples

Metabolism is controlled by the nervous system and hormones. The rate of metabolism increases to generate additional heat.

Heat loss effectors reduce the metabolic rate, promote sweating and bring blood to the skin surface.

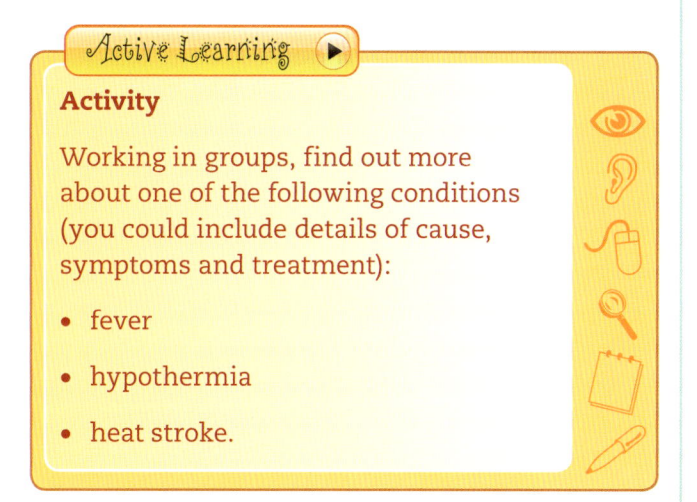

Active Learning

Activity

Working in groups, find out more about one of the following conditions (you could include details of cause, symptoms and treatment):

- fever
- hypothermia
- heat stroke.

Warm and cold blood

Internal temperature control is a feature of warm-blooded animals – birds and mammals. Many 'cold-blooded' animals adapt their behaviour in ways that help to raise their body temperature and thus increase their activity. Lizards and snakes warm up by basking in the morning sun. A beehive can include more than 50 kg of worker bees. One of their jobs is to control the temperature of a hive, keeping it at around 34 °C. They do this by beating their wings to generate heat or bringing water droplets into the hive to evaporate and cool it down – a process similar to sweating.

These worker bees help to control the internal temperature of the beehive.

Finding a perfect balance

Case 2: Water balance

👍 Humans cannot survive without water. Proper **hydration** is essential for our physical and mental well-being. Each day we normally take in the same volume of water as we lose in order to maintain stable body conditions.

Dehydration

The symptoms of dehydration, when we lose too much water, are headaches, fatigue and poor concentration. Dehydration can be a particular problem for children and the elderly and during exercise.

Dehydration is avoided by making sure that everyone drinks enough fluid each day.

The brain contains the control centre for water balance and the main effectors are the kidneys. Receptors in one part of the brain, the **hypothalamus**, detect the concentration of the blood and direct the pituitary gland to increase or decrease the level of a hormone, ADH, which in turn increases or reduces the volume of urine released by the kidneys.

Nerves that are buried in the walls of blood vessels detect blood pressure. The blood pressure falls during dehydration and this stimulates drinking while reducing urine production.

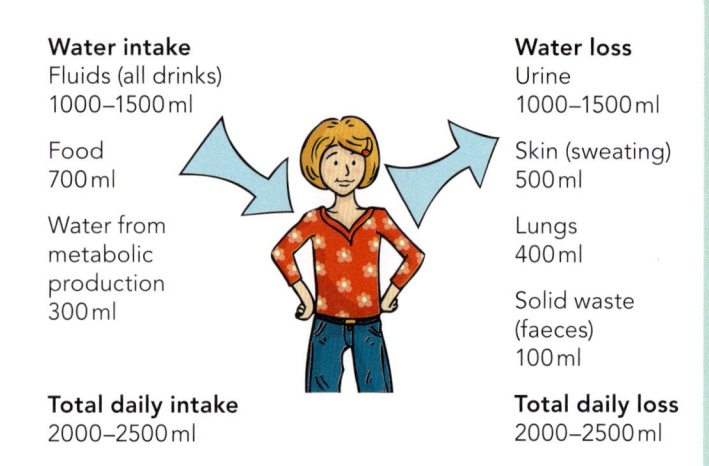

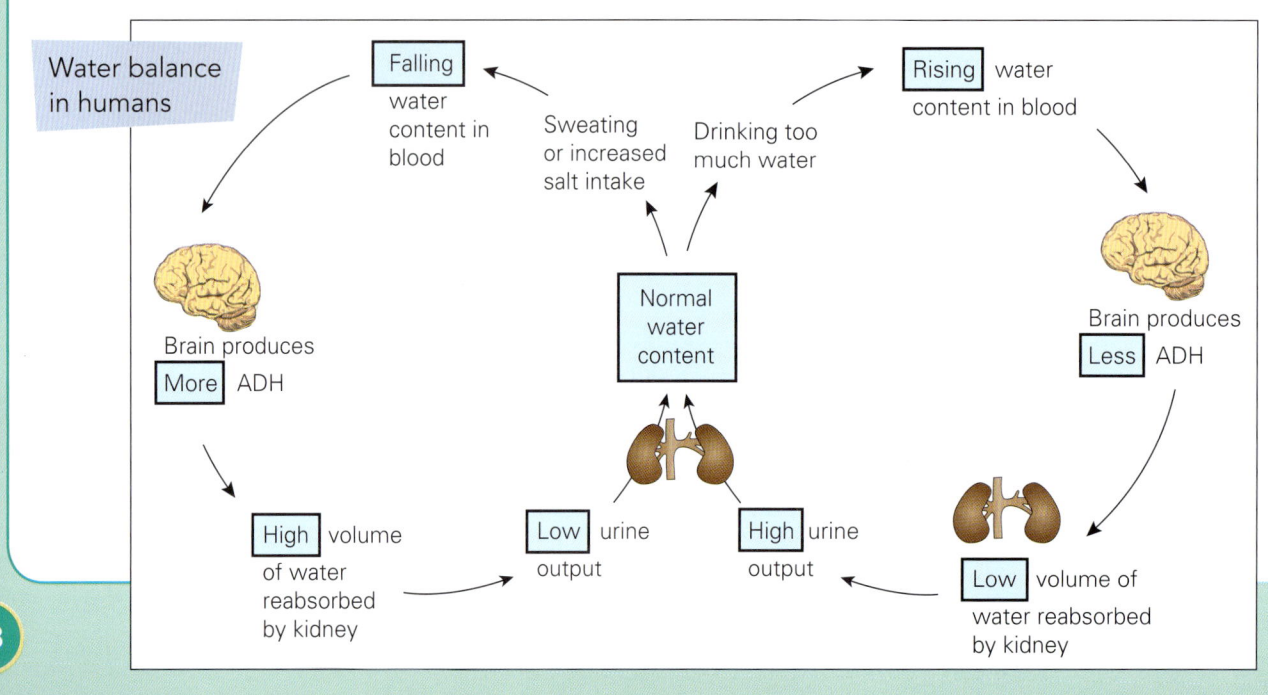

Water intake
Fluids (all drinks) 1000–1500 ml
Food 700 ml
Water from metabolic production 300 ml

Total daily intake 2000–2500 ml

Water loss
Urine 1000–1500 ml
Skin (sweating) 500 ml
Lungs 400 ml
Solid waste (faeces) 100 ml

Total daily loss 2000–2500 ml

Sports drinks often contain salts to replace those lost in sweat as well as sugars to boost energy.

Water balance in humans

Falling water content in blood → Brain produces More ADH → High volume of water reabsorbed by kidney → Low urine output → Normal water content

Sweating or increased salt intake / Drinking too much water

Rising water content in blood → Brain produces Less ADH → Low volume of water reabsorbed by kidney → High urine output → Normal water content

Finding a perfect balance

Case 3: Glucose balance

Glucose is a most important carbohydrate. We get glucose from digested food. Glucose is our main source of chemical energy because it is the raw material in aerobic respiration.

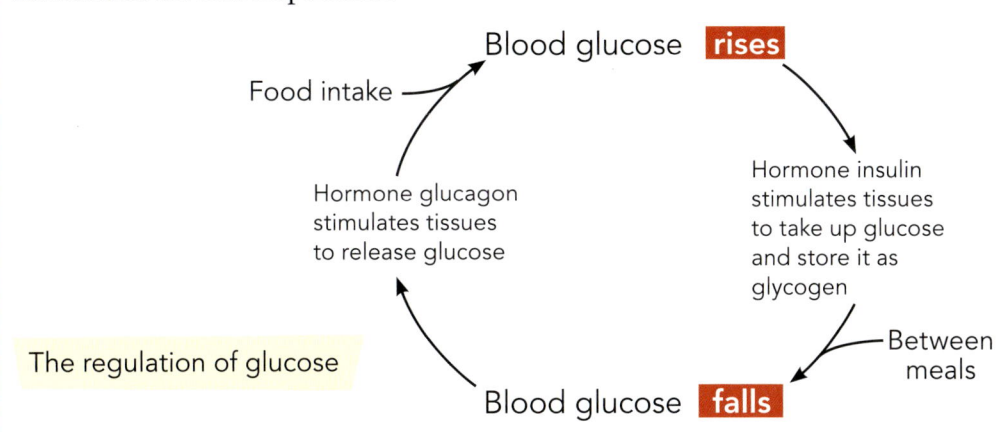

The regulation of glucose

- Food intake → Blood glucose **rises**
- Hormone insulin stimulates tissues to take up glucose and store it as glycogen
- Between meals → Blood glucose **falls**
- Hormone glucagon stimulates tissues to release glucose

Two hormones, **insulin** and **glucagon**, are involved in maintaining the balance of glucose in the blood. These are produced in **endocrine glands**. Glucose is dissolved in the blood but glycogen is insoluble. When the level of glucose in the blood gets too great, insulin stimulates the muscles and liver to take up glucose and convert it to glycogen for storage.

Constant demands are made on glucose by different parts of our body. However these demands are constantly changing.

Balance in our bodies is controlled in a number of ways.

Exercise and activity use glucose to release energy. Marathon runners and other endurance athletes often eat lots of pasta and other carbohydrates before a competition to boost the reserves of glycogen in their muscles and liver.

The **thyroid gland**, an endocrine gland, controls how quickly the body uses energy.

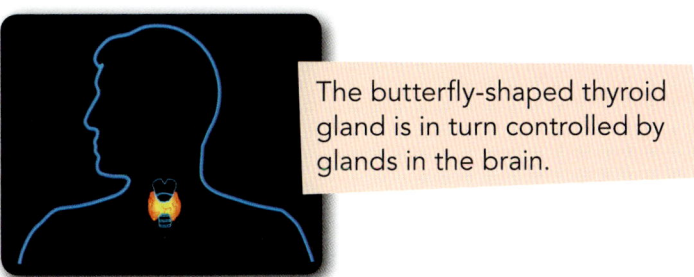

The butterfly-shaped thyroid gland is in turn controlled by glands in the brain.

Your brain works really hard. Although it makes up only 2% of your body mass, it receives 15% of the circulated blood and is responsible for 20% of total oxygen consumption and 25% of total body glucose utilisation.

Finding a perfect balance

Case 3: Glucose balance

Scientists are able to look at the activity of the brain as it carries out its work. CATSCAN and PET imaging can show that thinking takes place in different parts of the brain. The images and blood flow tell us that the brain is extremely active.

No wonder homework makes you hungry!

Adipose tissue, or body fat, is produced when excess carbohydrate exists in the diet. Childhood obesity is a significant issue that influences Scotland's health.

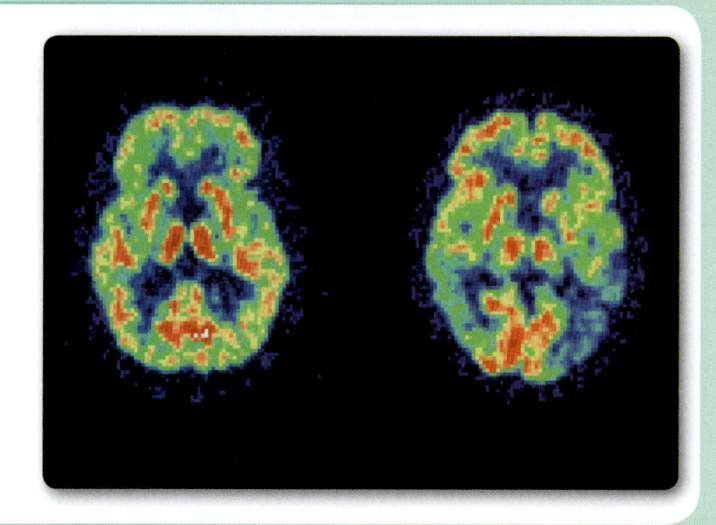

QUESTIONS

1. Construct a flow chart that shows the changes in blood concentration that take place in the lungs in response to exercise. (Use effectors, receptors and the control centre.)

2. Compare bee behaviour to sweating. (Use effectors, receptors and the control centre.)

3. This chapter showed you examples of temperature variation. Design an experiment that would show variation of pulse rate in the population. Think also about factors that will affect the pulse rate when the subjects are resting.

4. Describe what is meant by 'metabolic production of water'.

GLOSSARY

Adipose tissue Body fat

Endocrine glands Body glands that make hormones

Hydration Addition of water

Optimum Conditions in which the maximum response takes place

BIOLOGICAL SYSTEMS
Body Systems and Cells

6 Behave!

Level 3 — What came before?

● SCN 3-01a

I can sample and identify living things from different habitats to compare their biodiversity and can suggest reasons for their distribution.

Level 4 — What is this chapter about?

● SCN 4-12b

Through investigation, I can explain how changes in learned behaviour due to internal and external stimuli are of benefit to the survival of species.

Behave!

Innate or instinctive behaviour

Animals behave in particular ways to help them survive. Some behaviour is **innate**, has been inherited, and is often described as **instinct**. Other behaviour has been learned by the animal.

We show innate behaviour as soon as we are born – we instinctively know how to grasp and suckle.

Birds and insects are able to carry out long migrations instinctively. While some birds spend the summer in Scotland, such as swallows, others come here in the winter to live around our estuaries, like the pink-footed goose.

Honey bees respond instinctively to 'dances' that take place in darkness inside the hive that indicate the direction and distance of a food source.

Lots of animals, both vertebrates and invertebrates, have no contact with their parents yet their courtship and mating is successful. Such behaviour is instinctive and has not been learned through contact with other members of the species.

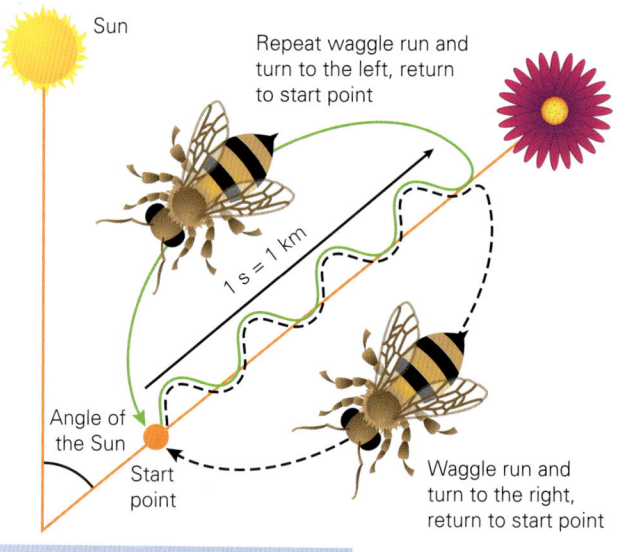

'Waggle dancing' in bees.

Fruit fly mating is instinctive.

Behave!

Training animals

Animals can be trained to do all sorts of things because the trainers understand animal behaviour. Most of us are familiar with training family pets. Draft animals are widely used around the world and make a significant contribution to agriculture.

Draft animals such as horses, mules or oxen are bred to carry out heavy work and they provide an alternative to tractors.

Trainers often use food treats to encourage particular behaviours.

Some animals can be trained to perform extraordinary things and can entertain us.

Most farm livestock, such as cattle, horses, sheep, pigs, hens and geese, show that they have learned lots about their environment. They learn where and when food and water will become available. They learn to recognise family members and others in their community and can discriminate between a range of environmental information.

Active Learning

Activity

Hungry snails will follow a trail of flour and water that is painted onto a Perspex sheet with a brush. Vary the proportions of flour and water in the trail to find the fastest snail in your tank.

Behave!

Behaviour and learning

Since animals can be trained, it is quite clear that they are capable of **learning**. Our learning is influenced by a number of internal and external factors. Think about the conditions that exist when you are learning something new.

Effective learning takes place when …

… they share each others' ideas

… they are not distracted

… they have slept well

… I can listen to my music

… I am allowed to eat

Active Learning

Activity

Design a school science laboratory that would improve learning/raise attainment.

Animal behaviour and survival

Animals' behaviour helps their survival by enabling them to avoid difficult conditions, deal with competitors or predators and find a mate. Some particular animal behaviours are described below.

Hibernation and aestivation

Hibernation is rare in British mammals. It is only seen in hedgehogs, dormice and all bat species. Amphibians and several other invertebrates carry out hibernation, including frogs and queen bumblebees. Worldwide lots of mammals are able to hibernate and avoid the extreme conditions of winter.

Hibernating animals are inactive and their **physiology** changes to lower their breathing and heart rate and so reduce overall energy use. Digestion and kidney filtration also slow down and the animal will only occasionally stir during a long hibernation.

Aestivation (east-iv-ay-shun) allows some animals to survive in hot places by adaptations that are designed to reduce water loss. Aestivation is similar in some ways to hibernation since it involves physiological adaptations that result in reduced metabolism, thus assisting survival. It also

Behave!

Animal behaviour and survival

involves behavioural adaptations, such as moving out of the heat of the Sun to find cooler, moister habitats.

Migration

Migration is a strategy that is used by many different kinds of animals so that they are always in favourable conditions. The world's greatest migration takes place each year when nearly two million wildebeest, zebras and other herbivores migrate through the Serengeti in East Africa looking for fresh grass and water. Predators such as lions and hyenas follow the herds.

The pink-footed goose breeds inside the Arctic Circle. The long days of the arctic summer ensure that they are able to raise and feed young geese so that they can all make the journey south to the milder winters in the UK. Around a quarter of a million of these birds spend the winter here around our estuaries, such as the Solway Firth, where they feed mainly on seeds and grass.

The pink-footed goose

Defence mechanisms

Many prey species have evolved **defence mechanisms** to aid their survival by protecting them from their predators. Successful defence strategies include fast running, kicking, biting and aggressive behaviour. Other animals have evolved protective spines and shells, such as hedgehogs and tortoises. Several species of lizard can lose their tails if they are grabbed by predators. The tail then grows back quite quickly.

Hover flies have evolved stripes to mimic the appearance of stinging bees and wasps and so defend themselves from predation.

Lots of animals taste unpleasant and have evolved bright colouration to warn off predators who have learned to avoid brightly coloured prey. The ladybird is an example. **Camouflage** is another frequently used approach that enables prey to hide in their habitat. Some animals have evolved to carry out a particular behaviour at the same time. This synchronisation of behaviour is intended to overwhelm predators. Mayflies, for example, all emerge from their pupae at the same time so that there are numerous adults mating and laying their eggs in water simultaneously. The mayfly larvae may then spend up to 3 years in the water.

Mayfly larvae

Behave!

Animal behaviour and survival

Courtship rituals

Courtship rituals take place in many animals prior to mating. Courtship behaviour is central to one of the most important ideas of the Theory of Evolution by Natural Selection. Charles Darwin's theory explains that survival of a species depends on their 'fitness'. This does not mean their physical strength, but refers to the organism being 'best adapted' to its environment and passing favourable genes on to subsequent generations.

Courtship rituals can stimulate all the senses and are mainly carried out by males. Vocal displays and breeding colours help males to attract mates. The early morning bird song – the so-called 'dawn chorus' – is very familiar during springtime.

Scents can also be used to attract mates. Some turtles court by brushing each other with their flippers.

In humans, kissing is an important part of courtship. Perfumes make us more attractive.

Three Nobel Prize winners

In 1973, three animal behaviour scientists won the Nobel Prize for Physiology or Medicine.

Karl von Frisch was an Austrian scientist whose careful observations of honey bee behaviour in and around their hives led to an understanding of their colour vision and the way that worker bees communicate the location of food to their fellow workers.

Konrad Lorenz was also Austrian and studied the behaviour of geese and chickens. He noted how newly-hatched birds 'imprint' onto a feature of their parent, enabling them to quickly follow them in nature, aiding their survival. He found that young birds could be encouraged to imprint onto a scientist in a laboratory and become dependent on them.

Nikolaas Tinbergen was a Dutch scientist who lived and worked in Oxford. Like Lorenz and von Frisch he carried out field observations of animal behaviour and linked behavioural stimuli to instinct.

These three scientists – von Frisch, Lorenz and Tinbergen – are considered to be the 'fathers of animal behaviour'.

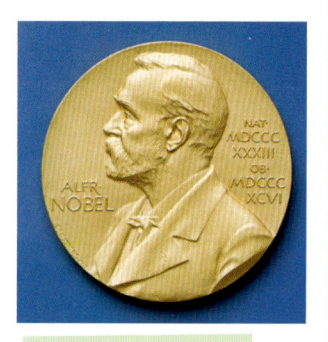

The Nobel Prize (medal)

Behave!

Choice chambers

Choice chambers allow you to investigate animals' preferences. They are often made from simple equipment such as plastic Petri dishes or glass tubing.

In this choice chamber four alternative conditions – combinations of light/dark and damp/dry – are offered to the animals and they will move to the most favourable conditions. Slaters (woodlice) are found under leaves and stones. Can you predict where they will move in this choice chamber?

Choice chambers can be used to investigate animals' preferences for physical conditions such as light, humidity, pH, soil texture etc. They can also be used to investigate food choices. You might try this experiment:

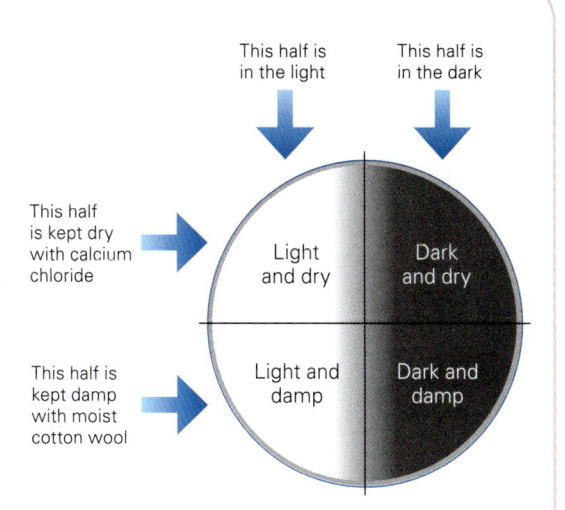

Active Learning

Activity

Use a cork borer to cut discs from pressed leaves such as oak, beech or holly.

Line a Petri dish with a circle of 5 mm squared paper.

Draw a line down the diameter of the squared paper.

Dampen the paper.

Place ten leaf discs on each half of the Petri dish.

Leave for three days in darkness and look for signs of predation by the slaters – signs that they have eaten the leaf discs and signs of their waste.

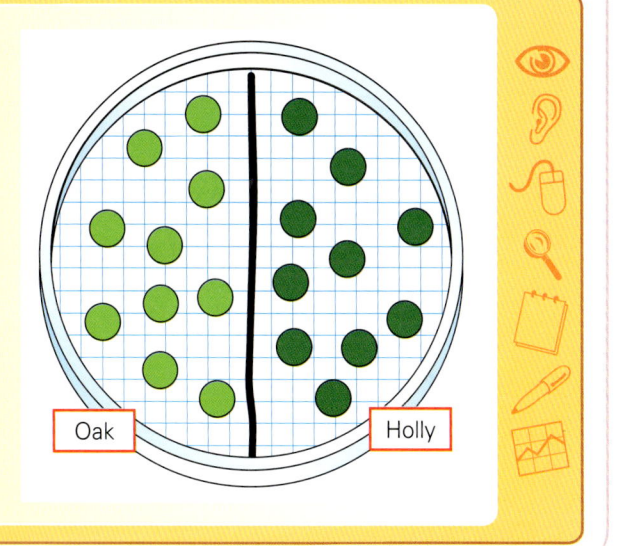

QUESTIONS

1. 'Fruit fly mating is instinctive.' Design an experiment that would test this statement.
2. Make a list of the advantages and disadvantages of using draft animals to farmers and to the animal.
3. What are your views on training animals? Find valid evidence to support your opinion.
4. Prepare a case study on a mammal that hibernates. Use library and Internet resources to support you.
5. Give examples of each sense being used in courtship rituals.
6. Prepare a mind map to summarise the survival mechanisms that are mentioned in the chapter.

GLOSSARY

Learning Change of behaviour as a result of practice, training or experience

57

BIOLOGICAL SYSTEMS
Body Systems and Cells

7
Cell growth and repair

Level 3 — What came before?

SCN 3-13a
Using a microscope, I have developed my understanding of the structure and variety of cells and of their functions.

SCN 3-14a
I understand the processes of fertilisation and embryonic development and can discuss possible risks to the embryo.

SCN 3-14b
I have extracted DNA and understand its function. I can express an informed view of the risks and benefits of DNA profiling.

Level 4 — What is this chapter about?

SCN 4-13a
By researching cell division, I can explain its role in growth and repair and can discuss how some cells can be used therapeutically.

Cell growth and repair

The nucleus

All processes that take place in the body's cells, including growth and repair, are controlled in the **nucleus**. The nucleus contains the genetic information that a cell must have in order to function.

The information within a cell is located on structures called **chromosomes** and is called the cell's **genetic code**. The genetic code acts like the cell's instruction manual. When new cells are made, it is essential that they each receive a complete copy of the instruction manual. Cells are able to copy their chromosomes before dividing into two new cells. Thus each new cell will receive an identical copy of the organism's genetic code.

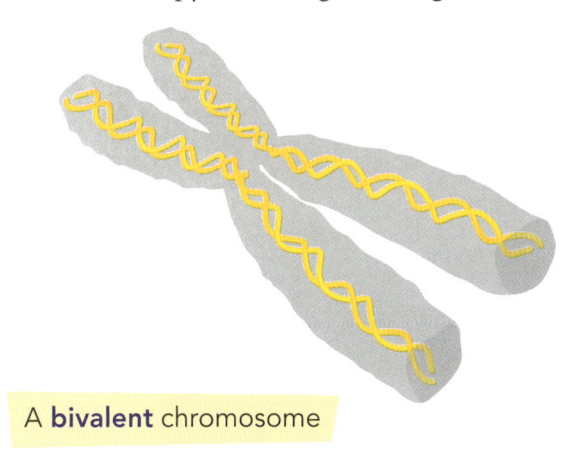

A **bivalent** chromosome

Human genetic code

The information needed by human cells is carried by 46 chromosomes. At fertilisation, each new human being receives 23 chromosomes from each of its parents.

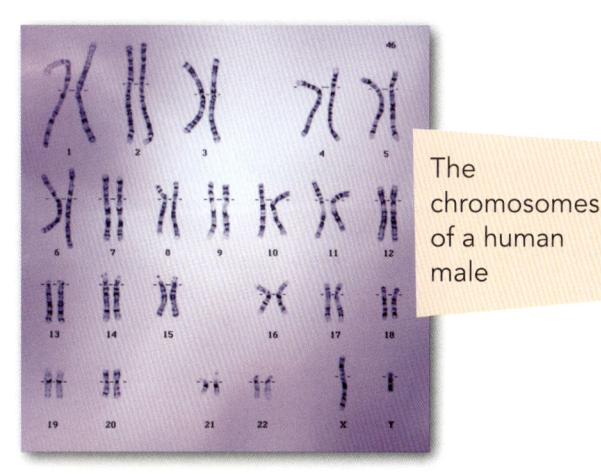

The chromosomes of a human male

Active Learning

Activity

Make a model of an organism's chromosomes as they would appear during **mitosis**. Assume the organism has eight chromosomes. (You could use card, wool and plasticine.)

Multiplication is the name of the game

Living organisms must be able to make new cells in order to grow and replace damaged cells. New cells are formed in a process called **cell division** in which each existing cell divides into two. Each new cell must have a nucleus containing an exact copy of all the genetic information.

Cell growth and repair

Multiplication is the name of the game

Before any cell starts to divide into two, it copies the genetic information in its nucleus. During cell division the genetic information will be used to make two identical nuclei. In the final stage of cell division, the cytoplasm will divide into two.

The main steps in cell division

Before cell division begins	The chromosomes inside the nucleus are copied (thus copying the genetic material, the DNA).
Stage 1 of cell division	The envelope around the nucleus disappears and the chromosomes in the cell become visible. The chromosomes arrange themselves across the centre of the cell. The two halves of the chromosome are then pulled to opposite ends of the cell.
Stage 2 of cell division	The nuclear envelope reforms around the chromosomes and the cytoplasm divides to form two new daughter cells.

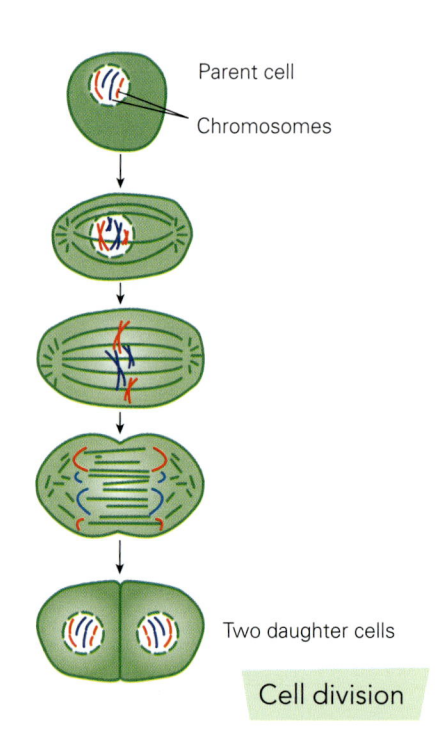

Parent cell
Chromosomes
Two daughter cells

Cell division

Growth in animals

The most rapid cell growth that takes place in humans and other mammals occurs when the embryo is developing in the womb. We all started life as just one cell that divided into two cells, then four and eventually into many millions of cells. These developed into specialised cells that formed the tissues, organs and systems of the human body that you were born with. All of these new cells were formed by the process of cell division.

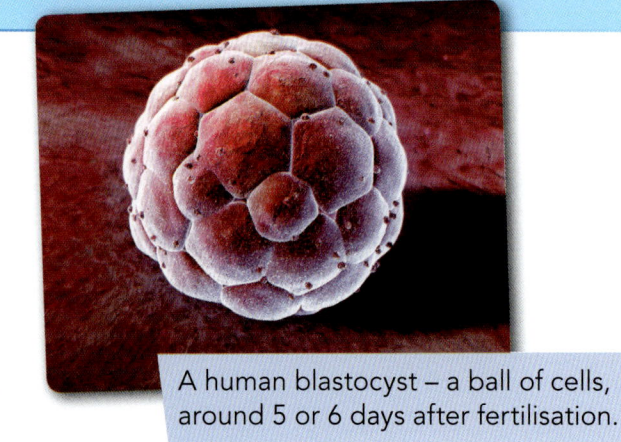

A human blastocyst – a ball of cells, around 5 or 6 days after fertilisation.

Growth continues from the time we are born as the systems of the body develop and mature. We get bigger due to growth of the skeleton and associated tissues. Even after we have reached our mature height we still continue to grow in the sense that we still produce new cells to replace old or damaged cells.

Cell growth and repair

Growth in flowering plants

Plant growth takes place in specialised tissues called **meristems**. Cells in the meristems divide rapidly into cells which then differentiate into particular tissues such as roots, transport vessels or photosynthetic cells.

New cells are produced by the meristems at the tips of the tree and this lets them grow taller; the meristems at the tips of the roots help trees to grow deeper into the soil. Meristems around the stem help to increase the tree's girth each year.

Active Learning

Activity

Each year a tree forms a new growth ring. It is suggested that they form because meristems are more active in the spring, so cell growth takes place at different rates at different times of the year. Examine tree rings closely with a hand lens and observe prepared microscope slides to find evidence to support that idea.

Repair in humans

The human body has an amazing ability to produce new cells and to heal itself. The repair of damaged tissues involves three main stages:

1. A clot forms and damaged cells are removed. This may last for a few days and the wound might be red and painful.
2. New cells are produced to replace the damaged tissue. They will not form an exact copy of the damaged tissue and a scar may form. This may take a few weeks.
3. The body continues to improve the new cells and the scarring begins to fade. This may take many years.

Repairing skin tissue

The skin acts as a protective barrier to infection. It is, therefore, important that the skin heals quickly when it is damaged. Small cuts will heal themselves within a few days as long as we are careful to keep the wound clean. Larger cuts can be helped to heal by the insertion of stitches that knit the edges of the wound together. This helps the skin to repair itself and reduces the chances of infection.

Cell growth and repair

Repair in humans

Broken bones

👍 At some point in our lives many of us may suffer an injury that damages a bone. Bones give us support and it is important that they are protected from weight bearing when they are healing. Putting the bone in a plaster helps the bone to heal, free from any stresses or strains. The gap in the damaged bone will be filled with new cells which will eventually form hard bone cells. The healed bone will be strong enough to have the plaster removed after 6 to 12 weeks, however the bone will continue to repair for years and eventually the line of the original fracture may not be visible in an X-ray.

Our skin, bones and blood are constantly being maintained as cells are replaced. If we break a bone or we cut ourselves, the damaged tissues will repair quickly, will eventually be replaced and the injuries will heal.

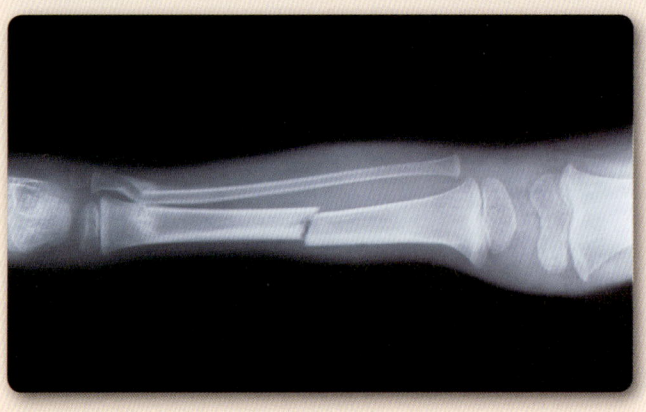

Rapid cell division and growth takes place to repair broken bones.

Skin is repaired by rapid cell growth. Wound healing is a very complicated process that involves many different cells and types of chemicals that circulate in the blood. The blood system contributes to the process with proteins, antibodies and white blood cells.

Blood cells

There are two main types of cells present in blood: red blood cells and white blood cells.

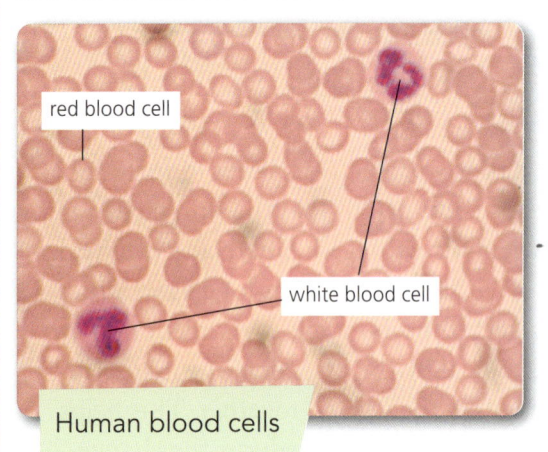

Human blood cells

Red blood cells have a very specific function: they transport oxygen from the lungs to the cells. White blood cells are part of our immune system. Their function is to attack and destroy disease-causing bacteria and viruses. There are different types of white blood cells that provide this protection.

As the blood travels through the body, red blood cells become damaged and must be replaced.

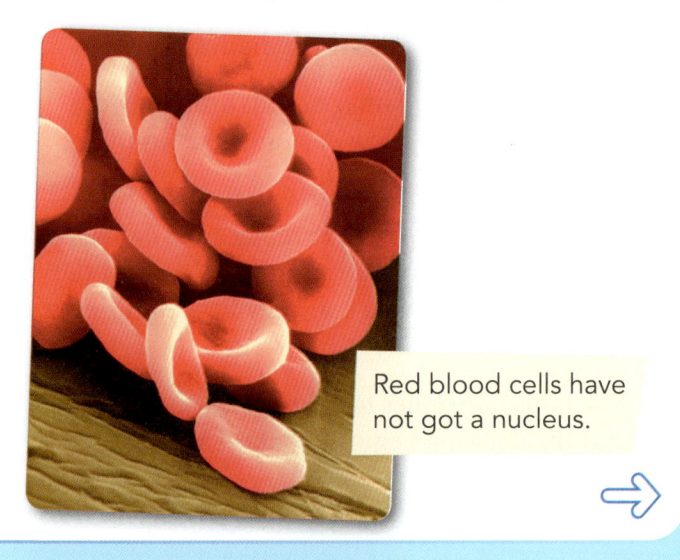

Red blood cells have not got a nucleus.

Cell growth and repair

Blood cells

Typically a red blood cell will live for only a few weeks. New red blood cells are formed from special cells in the bone marrow. In a lifetime we will replace our red blood cells many, many times. We can donate blood because the **stem cells** in the bone marrow are replacing our red blood cells continually.

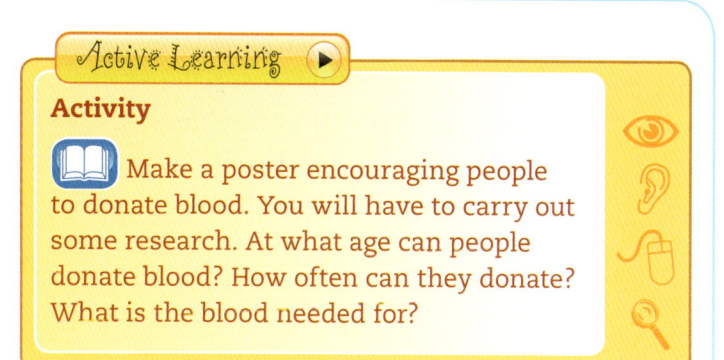

> **Active Learning**
>
> **Activity**
>
> Make a poster encouraging people to donate blood. You will have to carry out some research. At what age can people donate blood? How often can they donate? What is the blood needed for?

Stem cells

Stem cells are found in all plants and animals. They are produced by cell division and can specialise into a range of cell types.

Blood stem cells

Human blood is made in the bone marrow. The stem cells divide and then grow and specialise into the various types of blood cell. The proportions of the different cell types are controlled by hormones. One hormone, EPO, promotes red cell formation and can be used as a medicine for patients that have particular forms of anaemia and some cancers to help boost the red cell count.

There have been reported cases of endurance athletes, particularly marathon runners and long-distance cyclists, using EPO illegally to boost their performance. The resultant increase in red cells allows more oxygen to be carried to the muscles, enabling such athletes to train longer and harder.

This cyclist was stripped of his winning title in the Tour de France after failing a drug test.

Stem cells and the future

Stem cells can be used to grow many different types of cells and scientists are investigating the possible uses of these cells in the treatment of disease. In the future, stem cells could be injected into broken bones in order to speed up healing or used to help repair organs that have been damaged by disease. An example of this is the use of stem cells to help repair the damage the heart suffers after a heart attack.

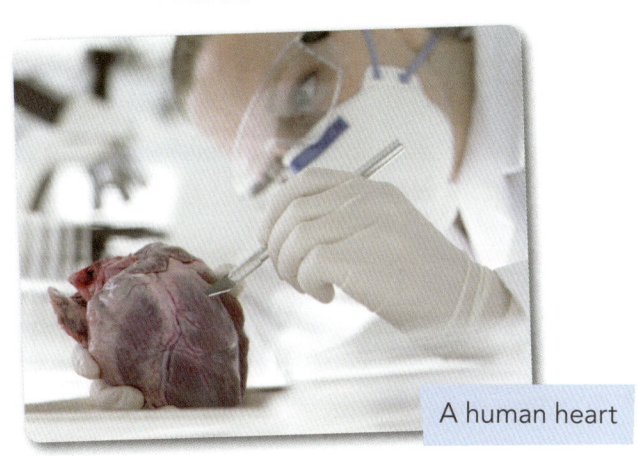

A human heart

One of the most exciting areas of research is the potential use of stem cells in the treatment of spinal cord injuries. These injuries leave people paralysed and stem cells could offer the possibility of a reduction in the amount of paralysis.

Cell growth and repair

Stem cells

However not everyone is in favour of the use of stem cells. This is because the stem cells are sometimes taken from living embryos. New developments may allow scientists in the future to grow stem cells from a person's own cells.

Active Learning

Activity

In a group, discuss whether you are in favour of or against stem cell research. If you are not sure, what other information would help you to make up your mind?

QUESTIONS

1. Look at the diagrams of dividing cells shown below. Can you place them in the correct order?
2. Can you suggest reasons why a cut in the skin will heal in a matter of days but it takes many weeks to heal a broken bone?
3. Which part of the cell contains the genetic information?
4. Name five types of cells.
5. How many new cells are formed after the process of cell division?
6. When and where might new cells form in the human body?
7. What is unusual about stem cells?

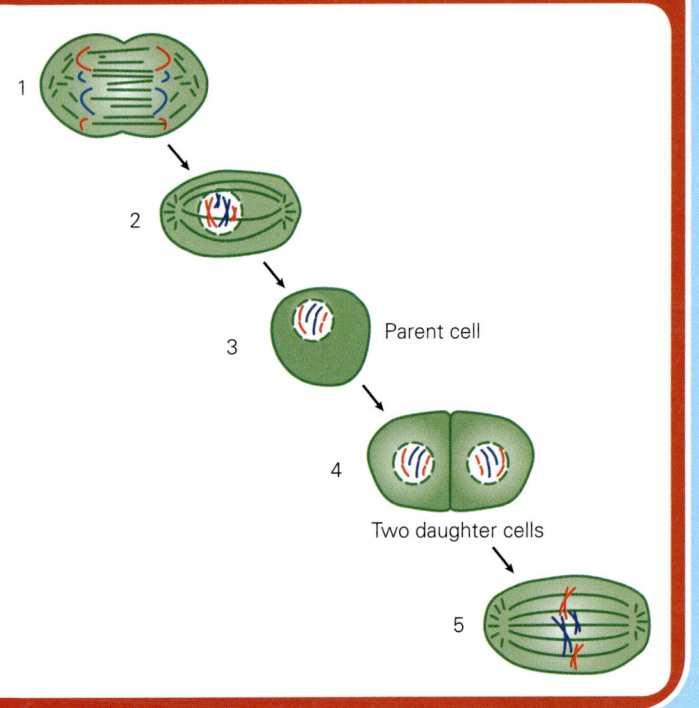

Parent cell

Two daughter cells

GLOSSARY

Bivalent Two parts

Meristem Plant growth tissue

Mitosis Cell division

Stem cell Unspecialised cell produced in rapidly dividing tissue

BIOLOGICAL SYSTEMS
Body Systems and Cells

8
Biotechnology

Level 3 — What came before?

SCN 3-13a

Using a microscope, I have developed my understanding of the structure and variety of cells and of their functions.

SCN 3-13b

I have contributed to investigations into the different types of micro-organisms and can explain how their growth can be controlled.

Level 4 — What is this chapter about?

SCN 4-13b

I have taken part in practical activities which involve the use of enzymes and micro-organisms to develop my understanding of their properties and their use in industries.

Biotechnology

Living factories

Cells are chemical factories. All living processes are controlled by chemical reactions which take place in cells. These chemical reactions occur very quickly because cells contain **enzymes**. Cells and the enzymes found within them can be used to manufacture useful materials. The cells of bacteria and fungi are especially useful.

Yeast industries

This reaction forms the basis of both the brewing industry and the baking industry.

Brewing and distilling

Most brewing is carried out using varieties of the yeast species *Saccharomyces cerevisiae*. Yeast grows naturally on the surface of fruits and helps the process of decay.

Alcohol can be produced from almost any source of sugar. Beer is made from maltose sugar, the product of starch digestion in germinating barley. Beer is often flavoured with hops. Wines are made from fruits, usually grapes.

Spirits like whisky and gin are made by preparing a simple fermentation and then distilling the alcohol to concentrate it.

The alcohol industry employs many people and whisky is one of Scotland's major exports.

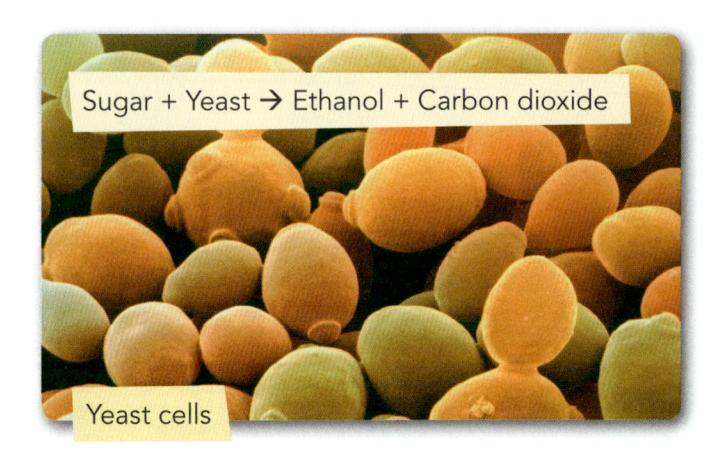

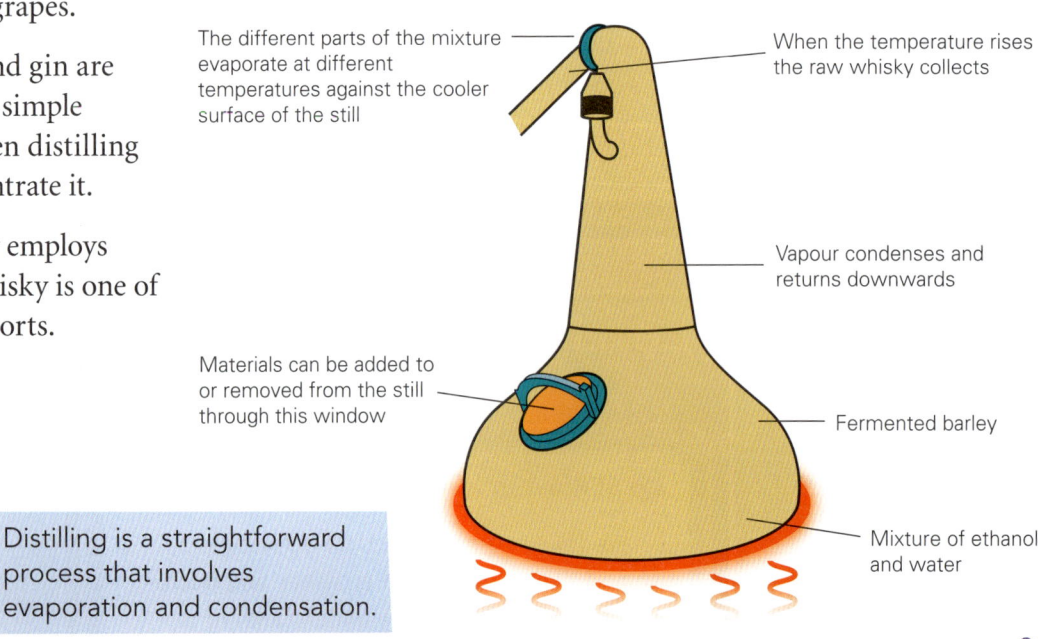

Sugar + Yeast → Ethanol + Carbon dioxide

Yeast cells

The different parts of the mixture evaporate at different temperatures against the cooler surface of the still

When the temperature rises the raw whisky collects

Vapour condenses and returns downwards

Materials can be added to or removed from the still through this window

Fermented barley

Mixture of ethanol and water

Heat

Distilling is a straightforward process that involves evaporation and condensation.

66

Biotechnology

Yeast industries

Baking bread

The carbon dioxide formed when yeast reacts with sugar is used in the baking industry to make bread rise. Bread is one of the most common **staple** foodstuffs in the world. Bread dough includes the following ingredients: flour, water, yeast, salt, oil and sugar.

The flour provides starch and gluten, a protein that provides the elastic properties of the dough as it rises and gives bread its 'spongy' texture. Sugar is added to supply a source of energy for the yeast which is unable to digest starch. Salt is added both for flavouring and to provide the correct environment for the yeast as it grows and respires.

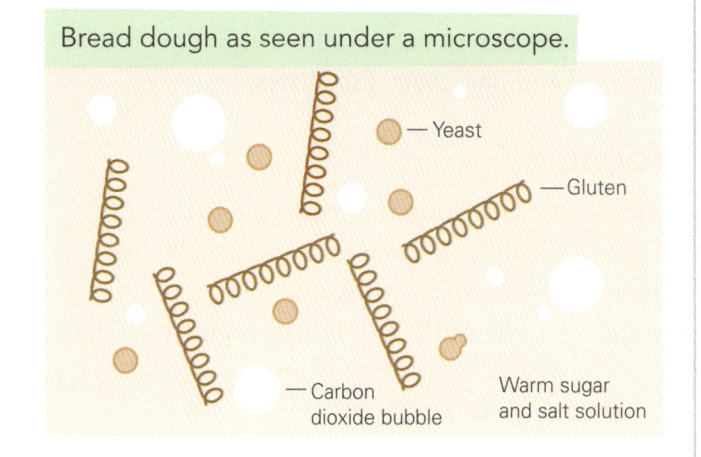

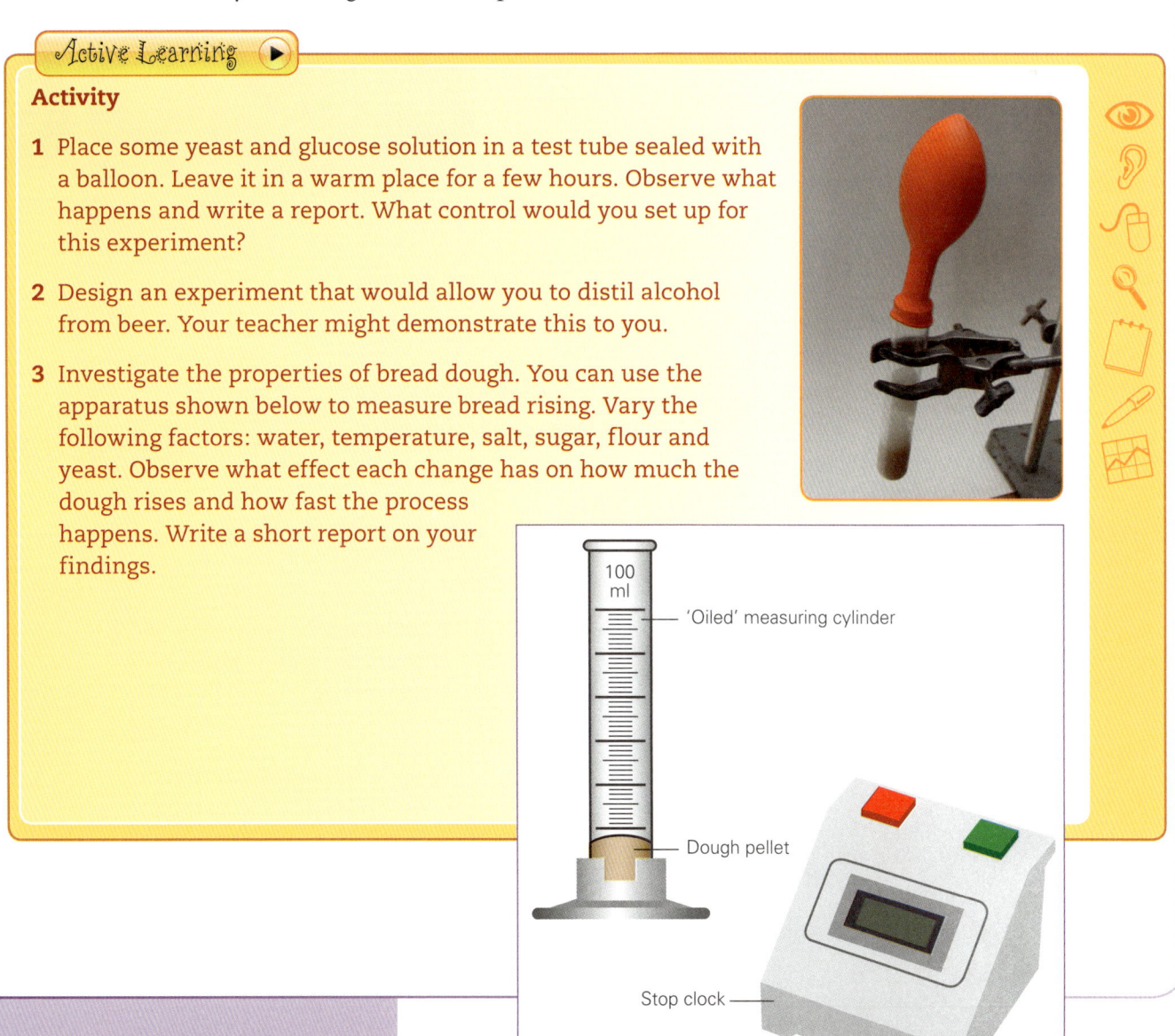

Bread dough as seen under a microscope.
— Yeast
— Gluten
— Carbon dioxide bubble
Warm sugar and salt solution

Active Learning

Activity

1. Place some yeast and glucose solution in a test tube sealed with a balloon. Leave it in a warm place for a few hours. Observe what happens and write a report. What control would you set up for this experiment?

2. Design an experiment that would allow you to distil alcohol from beer. Your teacher might demonstrate this to you.

3. Investigate the properties of bread dough. You can use the apparatus shown below to measure bread rising. Vary the following factors: water, temperature, salt, sugar, flour and yeast. Observe what effect each change has on how much the dough rises and how fast the process happens. Write a short report on your findings.

100 ml
'Oiled' measuring cylinder
Dough pellet
Stop clock

Biotechnology

Bacterial industries

The metabolism of bacteria can be used to provide useful materials, mainly in the food and pharmacy industries.

Yoghurt

Milk is carefully soured during yoghurt production. In the process, lactose sugar in the milk is converted into acid by bacteria. These micro-organisms change the taste of the milk and help to prevent growth of other bacteria that would spoil the milk. As a result, yoghurt has a longer shelf life than milk.

Cheese production

Most cheese is made from cows' milk but other cheeses can be made from the milk of other mammals, in particular sheep and goats. The process involves adding the enzyme rennin which coagulates the milk into solid curds and liquid whey. Bacteria are used to flavour the cheese. The cheese is then compressed to remove as much of the liquid whey as possible. Blue mould is sometimes added to cheese for added flavour.

All these products are made using micro-organisms.

Silage

Winter food for cattle often includes **silage**. Silage is prepared by harvesting grass several times during the growing season and packing it beneath waterproof materials, such as thick plastic sheeting. The silage remains wet and, in the absence of oxygen, bacteria release acids to 'pickle' the grass and thus preserve it. Sauerkraut (Sour-krowt) is pickled cabbage which is also preserved by acids released by bacteria.

Antibiotics

Blue mould in cheese is a fungus. Species of this mould gave the world its first **antibiotic**. Although there are now over 100 different types of antibiotics, development of new types of antibiotic continues all the time since bacteria mutate and become resistant to existing ones.

Active Learning

Activity

1 Ask your Home Economics teacher if you can prepare some yoghurt and some curds and whey in your next class.

2 Make a slide presentation on 'Fungi'. Your presentation can be about any aspect of fungi and must include five slides with suitable illustrations and information.

Biotechnology

Biological washing powders

Washing powders contain detergents to help clean our clothes. Biological washing powders contain added enzymes that are extracted from bacteria. The enzymes in the washing powder help to break down some of the chemicals that may stain our clothes, such as egg yolk or sweat.

The enzymes used in biological washing powders are unusual because they can function at high temperatures and are therefore still active even during a hot wash. These enzymes are extracted from bacterial cells that normally live in hot volcanic springs. Amylase enzymes remove starch-based materials. Protease enzymes can help to remove protein stains such as gravy or egg.

The products we use to wash our clothes can be biological or non-biological.

Active Learning

Activity

Biological washing powders do not mention the specific enzymes that they contain. Agar jelly can be used to investigate whether a particular biological washing powder contains proteases or not.

Use the apparatus shown to investigate the enzyme content of a biological washing powder.

Useful enzymes

Enzymes have been used in cheese production for hundreds of years. Enzymes are widely used in industry wherever precise chemical changes are required. They are used in food processing to release sugars from starch, to tenderise meat and to clarify fruit juices. Enzymes are even used to produce soft-centred chocolates. Biofuel and detergent production also involves enzymes. Contact lens cleaners contain protein-digesting enzymes to help prevent infections.

Enzymes are involved in DNA technology and are essential research tools, especially in genetic engineering and in pharmacology (medicine production).

Biotechnology

Useful enzymes

Medical uses of enzymes

Enzymes are used in medicine to treat blood clots and some types of tumour. The development of enzyme-based treatments can be difficult and expensive as enzymes can be hard to extract in a pure form from cells. Enzymes are also used in some diagnostic tests, such as testing for sugar in urine to help diagnose diabetes.

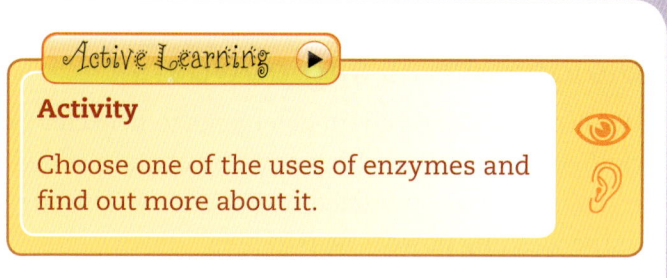

> **Active Learning**
>
> **Activity**
>
> Choose one of the uses of enzymes and find out more about it.

Gene therapy

Inherited diseases frequently involve faulty genes. **Gene therapy** involves the use of viruses to carry corrective genes into patients.

People with the genetic disease cystic fibrosis (CF) lack the correct genetic information and their lungs become clogged by sticky mucus. Treatment involves daily physiotherapy to dislodge the mucus. It is a serious inherited disease which shortens the lives of sufferers.

Experimental approaches in gene therapy have been used to treat cystic fibrosis. Scientists have attempted to deliver DNA into the cells of a CF patient using a virus as a **vector** (carrier).

Viruses were used for this purpose because they are able to invade cells. Normally when they do this they cause disease, so scientists developed virus vectors that would carry information but not cause disease. The safety of introducing viruses to

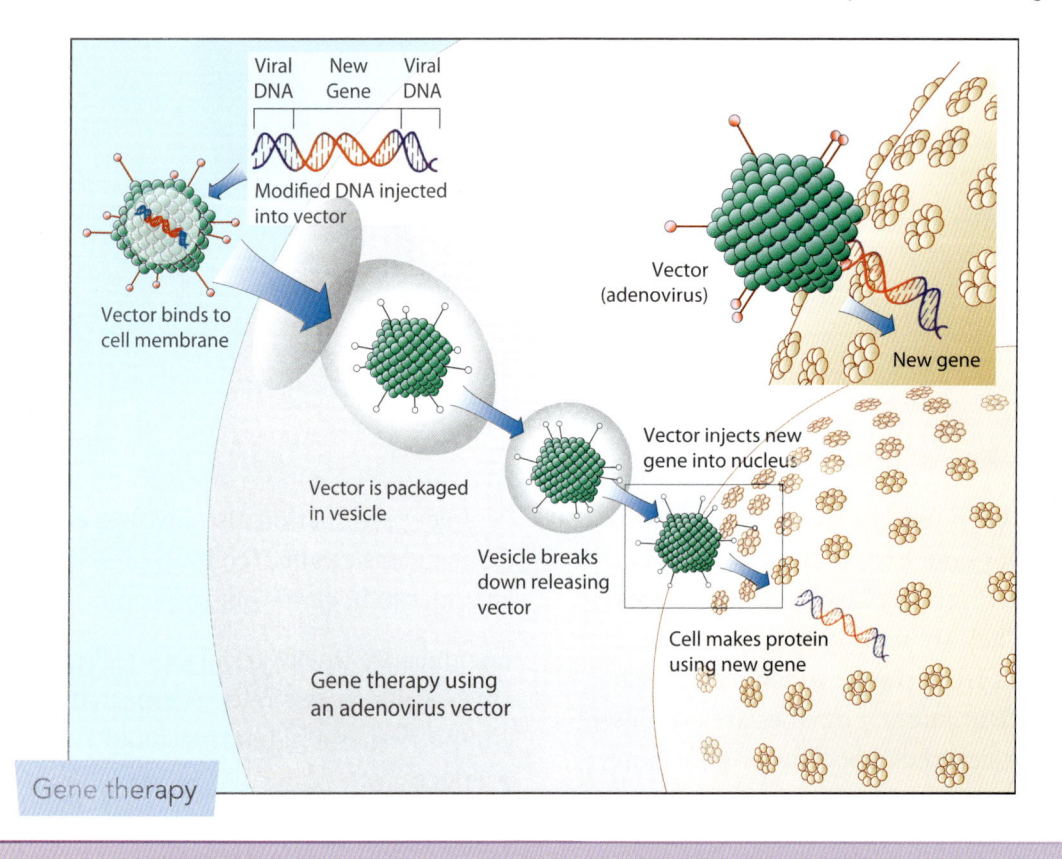

Gene therapy using an adenovirus vector

Gene therapy

70

Biotechnology

Gene therapy

the lungs of individuals who were already very ill was a cause for concern among the scientific team. What if the virus vector caused disease? What if the individual's immune system attacked the virus?

Gene therapy is still causing debate but new therapies are being developed all the time for diseases such as Parkinson's disease. Once the difficulties regarding safety have been overcome it may, in the future, be a very useful treatment for many diseases.

Active Learning

Activity

Carry out some further research into viruses. How do viruses reproduce? What diseases are caused by viruses? How big are viruses compared to other cells?

Present your research as a poster.

Nanotechnology

Nanotechnology is an exciting area of modern science which is often mentioned in the news. Nanotechnology refers to technology that happens at an atomic or molecular scale, generally between 1 and 100 **nanometres**.

'Nano-biotechnology' refers to the applications of nanotechnology to biological systems.

Scientists are regularly confronted with new infections that are brought about as the result of the evolution of drug-resistant bacteria, such as MRSA. Infection is also the cause of death in half of all people who die from burns. Researchers are applying nano-biotechnology to making an advanced wound dressing which will detect when a wound or burn is infected by bacteria, automatically release an antimicrobial agent to fight the infection and change colour to alert the patient and medical staff clinicians.

'Nanoparticles' are being engineered so that they are attracted to diseased cells and deliver drugs to specific cells (such as cancer cells).

In the future 'nanorobots' may repair diseased cells in a similar way to antibodies.

QUESTIONS

1. Find out the names of four different plants that are grown as staple crops around the world.
2. For each staple crop, make a table to show which part of the world it is grown in, the type of plant it comes from and any other uses that can be made from it.
3. Name the chemicals that speed up the chemistry of living organisms.
4. Find out the differences that exist in the ingredients of biological and non-biological washing powders or liquids.
5. Immunisation involves increasing immunity against particular diseases. Name three immunisations that are used against viruses.

GLOSSARY

Gene therapy Using DNA to treat inherited diseases

Nanometre One thousand millionth of a metre; 10^{-9} metres; 1/1 000 000 000 m

Nanotechnology Science that takes place at atomic and molecular scales

Staple The main source of energy and nutrients in the diet

Vector A carrier

BIOLOGICAL SYSTEMS
Body Systems and Cells

9
Reproduction and animal life cycles

Level 3 — What came before?

SCN 3-13a
Using a microscope, I have developed my understanding of the structure and variety of cells and of their functions.

SCN 3-13b
I have contributed to investigations into the different types of micro-organisms and can explain how their growth can be controlled.

SCN 3-14b
I have extracted DNA and understand its function. I can express an informed view of the risks and benefits of DNA profiling.

Level 4 — What is this chapter about?

SCN 4-14a
Through investigation, I can compare and contrast how different organisms grow and develop.

SCN 4-14b
Through evaluation of a range of data, I can compare sexual and asexual reproduction and explain their importance for survival of species.

Reproduction and animal life cycles

Reproduction

Reproduction is one of the essential characteristics of living organisms. All species of living organisms are able to produce offspring. Single-celled organisms such as bacteria are able to reproduce very quickly by dividing into two cells in a type of reproduction called **binary fission** (splitting into two). This type of reproduction is called **asexual** as it only involves one parent. Reproduction in plants can be **sexual** or asexual. (See Chapter 2 for more on plant reproduction.)

Reproduction in multicellular organisms such as flowering plants and vertebrates takes much longer as they reproduce sexually. This involves specialised sex cells (gametes) joining together.

This whole process can take weeks or months and, in some species, years.

The story of how a particular species reproduces is called its **life history**. There are many different life histories. Some animals use '**external fertilisation**' where the sex cells meet outside the female's body and sperms swim through water. Other animals have **internal fertilisation** and the male sex cell is placed inside the female's body during mating. All land animals have this type of fertilisation.

Some invertebrates may be maintained in the school laboratory and you will be able to study their life cycle.

The life cycle of the brine shrimp

Many pet shops can supply **cysts** of the North American brine shrimp, *Artemia salina*. The cysts are the dormant stage of the life cycle of the brine shrimp. They are very small (approximately 0.25 mm in diameter) and easily crushed, therefore they must be handled with care.

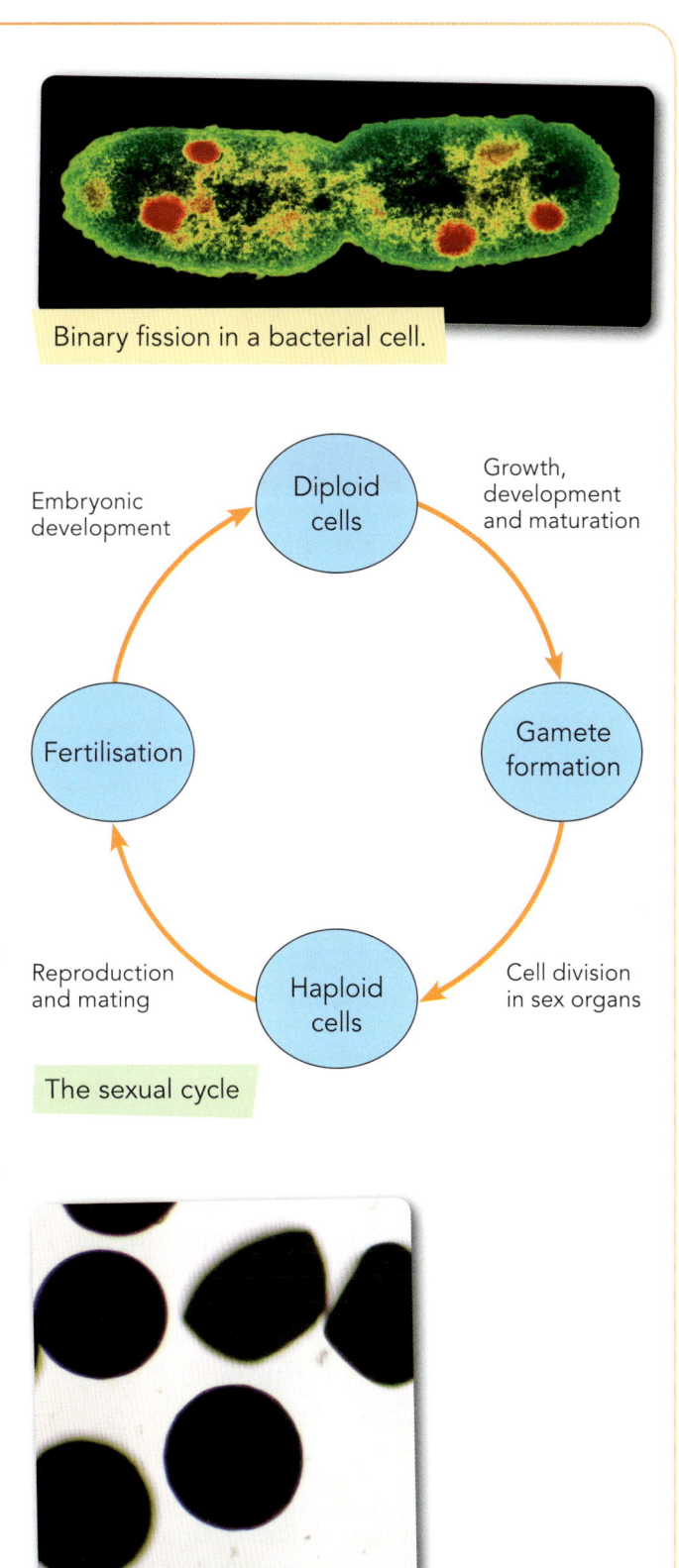

Binary fission in a bacterial cell.

The sexual cycle

Brine shrimp cysts

Reproduction and animal life cycles

Reproduction

To observe hatching, some cysts should be added to aerated salt water.

Hatched cysts form larvae called nauplii (now-plee) and it is possible to observe the effects of varying a number of environmental factors on the rate of hatching and development of the larvae.

A control group of cysts should always be maintained to provide a comparison.

Factors to be investigated may include:

- temperature
- light intensity
- salinity (salt concentration)
- oxygen levels
- exposure to environmental pollutants
- pH.

The eggs are fertilised inside the female and the zygote rapidly develops into a ball of cells.

Before being released from the brood sac into the environment, each embryo is surrounded by a protective capsule. This is the cyst. Approximately 4000 unspecialised cells are present at this stage. Cysts contain no water and are capable of surviving for very long periods of time even when frozen, heated to 80 °C, exposed to low air pressures or placed in dry environments. When the cyst is exposed to water, the process of embryo development restarts. Hatching of the larvae occurs approximately 24–48 hours later.

Hatching of a shrimp larva.

Male brine shrimps can be identified by the presence of large claspers.

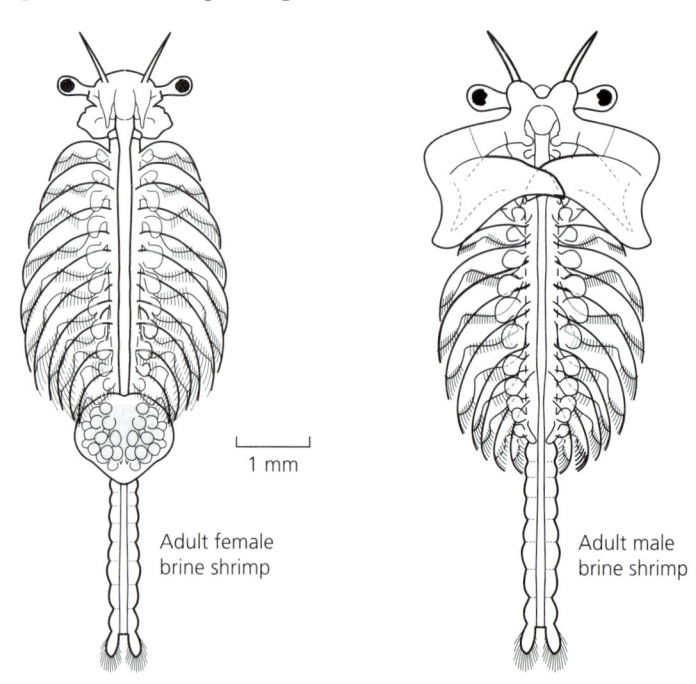

Male and female brine shrimps look different.

74

Reproduction and animal life cycles

Mating brine shrimps

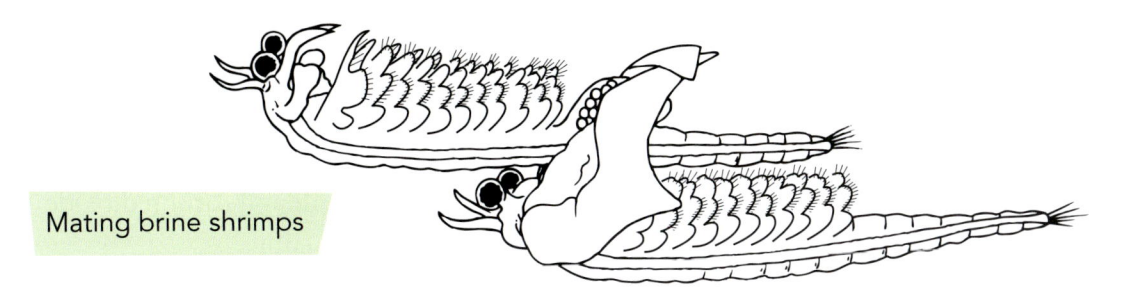

During the mating process, sperm are deposited inside the female and internal fertilisation takes place. Sometimes females can produce female offspring without the need for the presence of males. (Asexual reproduction of this type is fairly common in invertebrates, insects in particular.) The resulting offspring are clones of the parent.

The rate of reproduction can be very high and batches of eggs may be produced every few days. Some fertilised eggs have thin protective shells and hatch into larvae straight away. Other fertilised eggs with thick protective coatings dry out and remain inactive as a cyst.

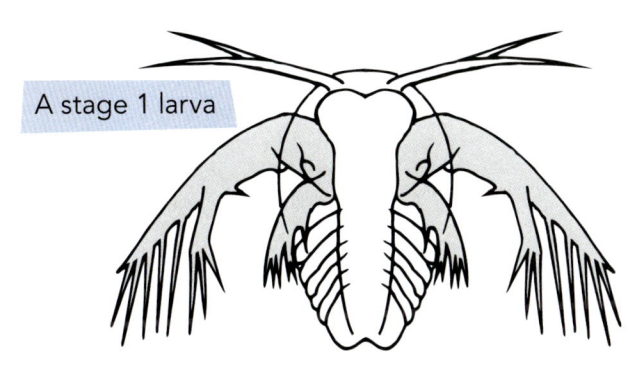

A stage 1 larva

After hatching, the larvae are 0.4–0.5 mm in length. They are brown-orange in colour due to the presence of a yolk sac which provides them with food. The larvae can swim and consist mainly of a head with two pairs of antennae and a pair of jaws sticking out of the head. The head has a visible mouth structure.

The lower portion of the larva has not formed at this stage. The digestive system of the larva is not completely developed either at this stage and as a result it does not feed from the environment, relying instead on its yolk sac for nourishment.

The larva will swim for 12–20 hours depending on the temperature of the water and will then moult into a second stage larva. At this stage it is around 0.6 mm in length and the lower portion of the larva starts to develop further. It is able to swim more strongly using its second antennae. It begins to filter feed on bacteria, algae and fragments of decaying life found in the water.

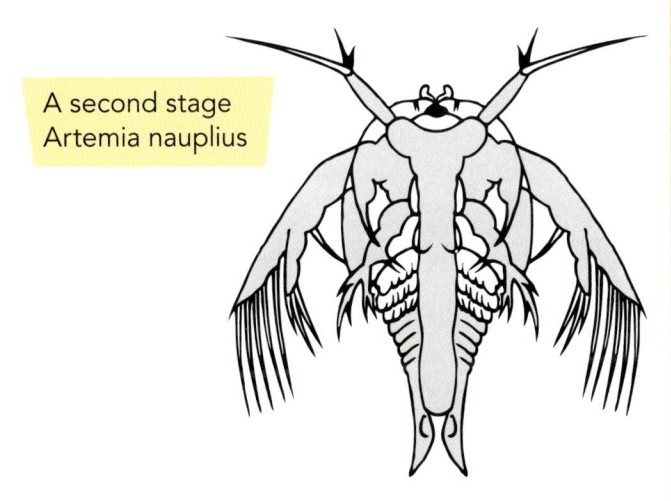

A second stage Artemia nauplius

The larva now undergoes a number of stages during which its eyes and lower body develop more fully. Before the final adult stage is reached, approximately seventeen different stages in development have been identified, including the addition of more body parts and the formation of reproductive organs.

Reproduction and animal life cycles

Reproduction

Adult brine shrimps

8 mm in length and may live for approximately 4 months. Some limbs act like paddles and push water backwards thereby propelling the organism forwards. Gills on certain limbs allow gas exchange – oxygen is taken in and carbon dioxide is released from the brine shrimp.

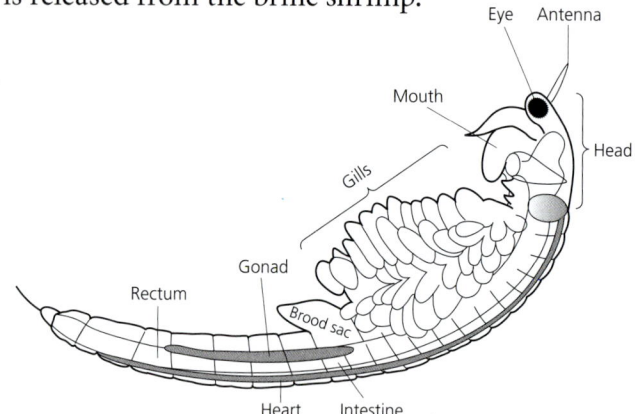

The adult shrimp stage is reached approximately 21 days after hatching. The shrimp's body mass has increased 500 times since it was a larva in the first stage of development. An adult shrimp is about

Active Learning

Activity

Research the growth and development of one animal using library and Internet resources. Use the four stages of a life cycle to provide the structure for a presentation. Try to include answers to each of the following questions:

- Which organism are you studying?
- Does your organism reproduce asexually or sexually?
- Do differences exist between males and females?
- Is fertilisation external or internal?
- How many eggs are produced?
- Where do eggs get fertilised?
- How many sperm cells are produced?
- Is development of the embryo internal or external?
- Do the young appear similar or different during all the stages of development?
- What protection or care is provided to the newborn?

You may choose any animal, but here is a list of possible choices:

Stick insect	Trout
Drosophila	Frog
Honey bee	Dog
Butterfly	Cat
Earthworm	Snake
Goldfish	Chicken/Hen

It may be possible to monitor the development of some of the invertebrates in the laboratory as long as you wash your hands before and after handling, take care and treat the animals with respect.

Reproduction and animal life cycles

QUESTIONS

1. Draw the life cycle of one of the following to show its key stages:

   a) daffodil
   b) fly
   c) brine shrimp.

   Use the picture below as a guide.

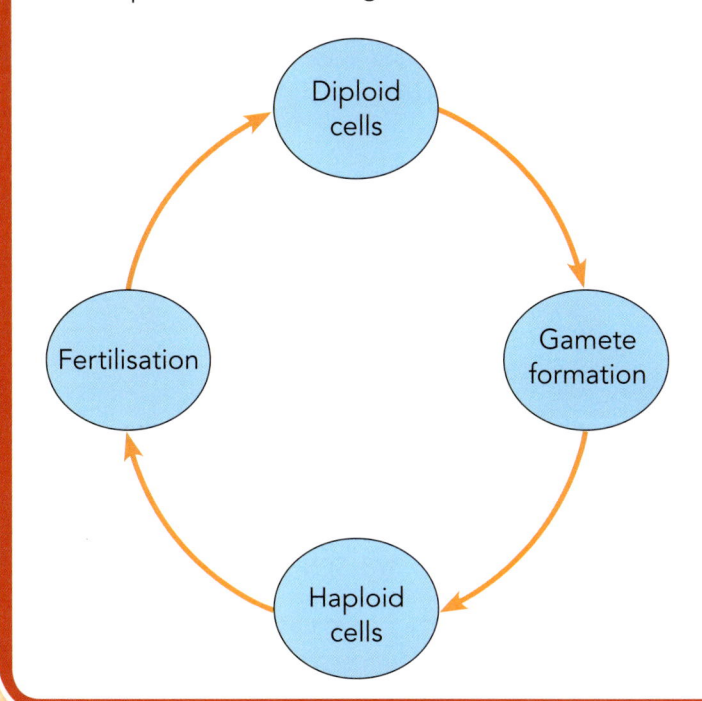

   Diploid cells → Gamete formation → Haploid cells → Fertilisation → Diploid cells

2. If a single bacterial cell divides by binary fission once every 20 minutes, how many bacteria will be produced by this cell:

   a) after 3 hours
   b) after 6 hours
   c) after 12 hours?

   What factors might limit the multiplication of this bacterial colony?

GLOSSARY

Asexual Increase in population that has resulted from one parent and therefore no sexual contact. The offspring are identical to the parent

Cyst Dormant (resting) stage of life cycle; often covered with a protective coat

Sexual Increase in population that has resulted from two parents and the exchange of sex cells. The offspring are genetically unique

77

BIOLOGICAL SYSTEMS
Inheritance

10 Inheritance

Level 3 — What came before?

SCN 3-12a
I have explored the structure and function of organs and organ systems and can relate this to the basic biological processes required to sustain life.

SCN 3-14a
I understand the processes of fertilisation and embryonic development and can discuss possible risks to the embryo.

SCN 3-14b
I have extracted DNA and understand its function. I can express an informed view of the risks and benefits of DNA profiling.

Level 4 — What is this chapter about?

SCN 4-14c
I can use my understanding of how characteristics are inherited to solve simple genetic problems and relate this to my understanding of DNA, genes and chromosomes.

Inheritance

DNA, genes and chromosomes

Inheritance is controlled by a chemical, **DNA**, which is found inside cells. DNA is a shortened form and its full name is **d**eoxyribo**n**ucleic **a**cid. DNA is a nucleic acid. DNA contains the genetic instructions for an organism – the complete plan for each living thing. We can easily extract DNA from cellular materials with common household materials – salt, washing-up liquid and alcohol.

DNA is found inside **chromosomes** – these are visible when cells divide in growing tissues. Humans normally have 46 chromosomes. Cats have 38 chromosomes, dogs have 78, barley has 14 and onions have 16 chromosomes.

Humans have around 30 000 **genes**, fruit flies around 13 000 genes and yeast around 6000 genes. The genes are joined together in a particular order along the chromosomes, rather like beads in a necklace. Each gene contains the code for a single inherited character such as eye colour, hair colour or blood type.

The DNA double helix is one of the world's most familiar scientific images. Its discovery led to a huge increase in the research carried out in several fields, most significantly in molecular biology, biotechnology and forensic science.

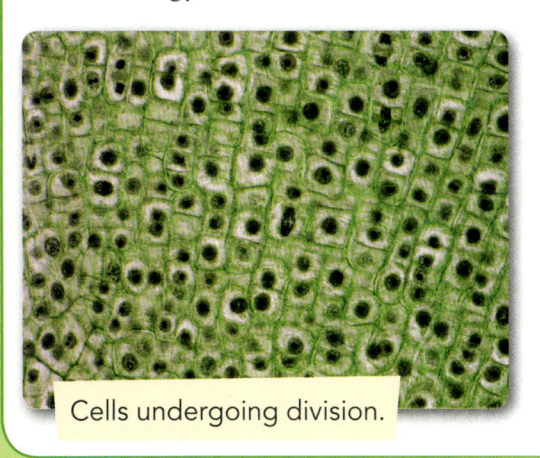

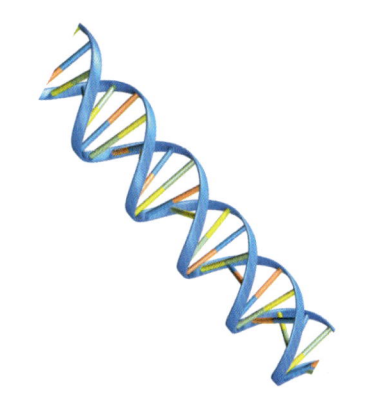

Cells undergoing division.

Each DNA molecule includes a sequence of **nucleotide bases** – abbreviated to A, T, G and C – which are the chemical code for each gene.

Active Learning

Activity

Look at some actively dividing cells from the tip of an onion or garlic roots which have had the nucleus stained. (**Safety** – if you are carrying out the staining, take great care. The stains are poisonous and must be handled carefully.) Under the microscope, try to see the following:

- new cells that are the result of division (A)
- chromosomes that are being pulled apart towards the ends of the cell to make new cells (B)
- tangled chromosomes becoming organised within dividing cells (C).

Inheritance

DNA, genes and chromosomes

DNA profiling (sometimes called genetic fingerprinting) is a technique that is widely used in science laboratories and allows the identification of the genes that are present in a sample. Since the results of the Human Genome Project were published in 2003, scientists have a reference library of all human genes. The complete gene sequence for several other micro-organisms, plants and animals have been completed, including mice, fruit flies and yeast.

Understanding genes is important in lots of areas of science. Cancer research, gene therapy, genetically modified organisms and cloning are all areas that are being researched in laboratories around the world. Many people find some of these areas controversial arguing that scientists are 'playing God'. Other people say that many of the arguments are emotional, misinformed and are not based on accurate scientific data.

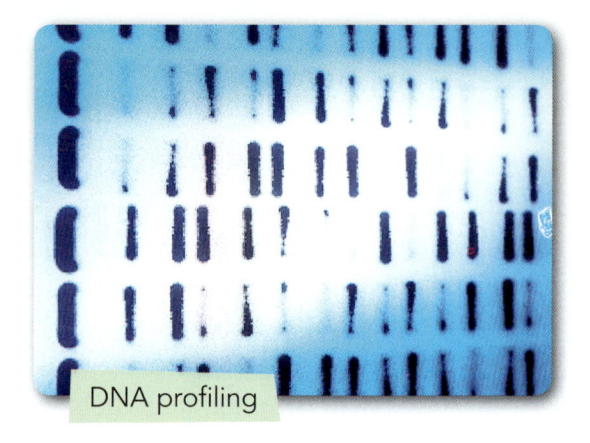

DNA profiling

Genes can also be helpful in historical research. Gene profiling is increasingly being used in historical research to identify the remains of people who died, often centuries ago.

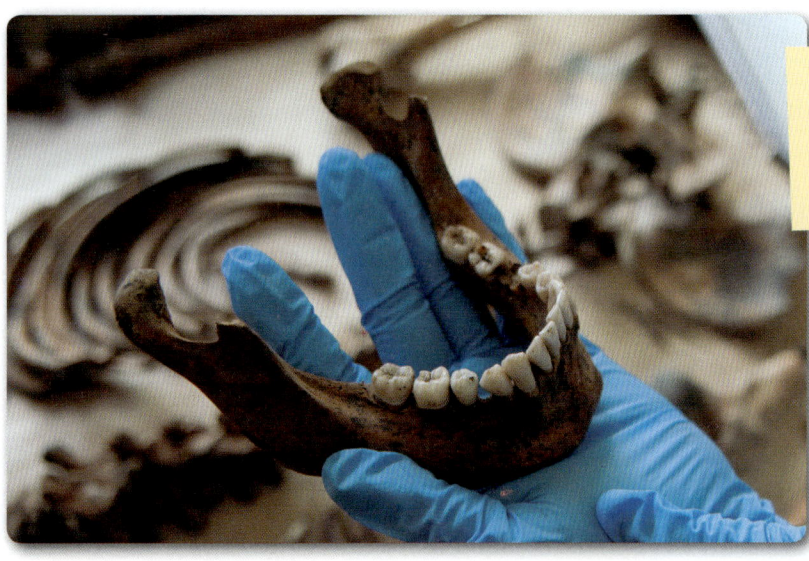

'Cold Case' teams research the causes of death in ancient skeletons. They use gene profiling to help identify the remains.

Active Learning

Activity

Perform research into genetic modification with library and Internet resources. List points for and against genetic modification.

How characteristics are inherited

Living things inherit their **characteristics** from their parents. Sexual reproduction involves the nuclei of sex cells or **gametes** (for example, sperms and ova in animals and pollen and ovules in flowering plants) joining together. One set of chromosomes is passed on from each gamete.

Gametes are special – you already know that sperms are able to swim (they are **motile**) and ova contain a food store.

Each of these types of cell is also unusual because they contain one set of chromosomes only. (Normal body cells, **somatic** cells, have two sets of chromosomes.) Gametes are produced in the sex organs by a special form of cell division that separates the chromosome pairs. If this was not the case the number of chromosomes would double every time reproduction took place.

'**Ploidy**' refers to the number of chromosome sets in a cell. Gametes with one set (n) are called **haploid** and zygotes with two sets (2n) are **diploid**. The cells that are produced from the zygote are diploid. When the individual reaches sexual maturity, it starts to produce gametes and the life cycle continues.

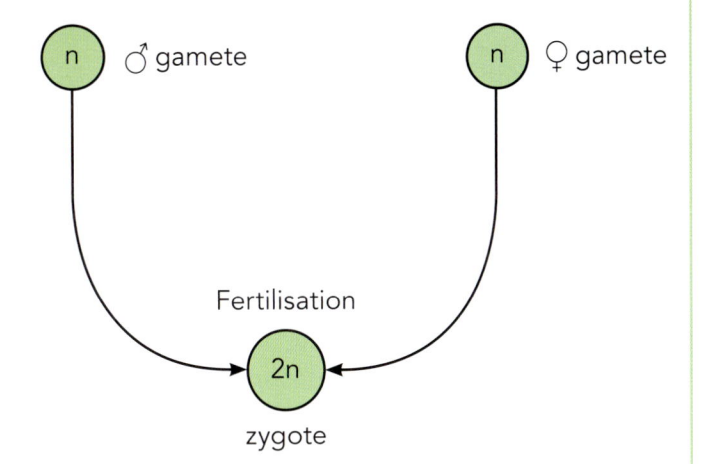

n – number of chromosomes
♀ – symbol used to represent female parent
♂ – symbol used to represent male parent

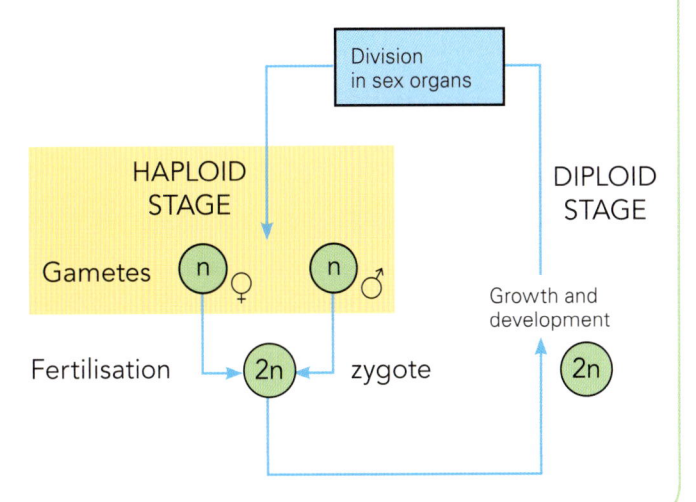

Inheritance

Polyploidy

Some animals and lots of plant species possess multiple sets of chromosomes.

Modern wheat started to evolve in the Middle East around 11 000 years ago but the process was helped by early farmers who chose the 'best' seeds and steadily 'improved' the crops. Larger seeds with increased yields have resulted from **polyploidy**. Wheat has strains that are diploid (two sets of chromosomes), **tetraploid** (four sets of chromosomes, with the common name of durum or macaroni wheat) and **hexaploid** (six sets of chromosomes, with the common name of bread wheat).

The emergence of civilisation has been closely associated with the cultivation of crop plants and animal breeding. Farming reduced the need for 'hunter gathering' and led to the establishment of villages and towns.

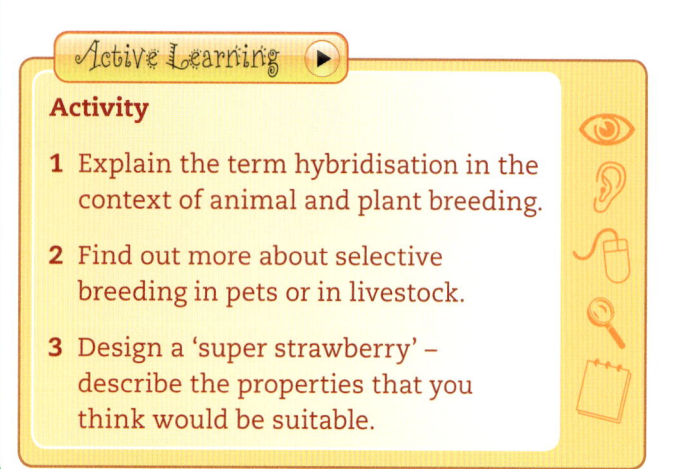

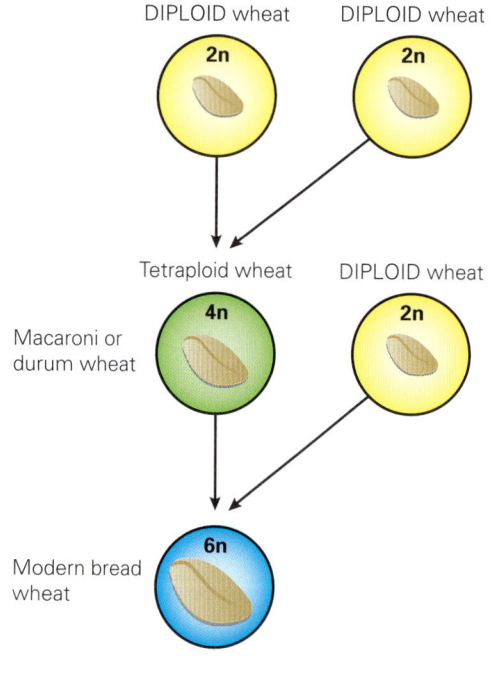

A seed head of a wheat plant

DIPLOID wheat 2n
DIPLOID wheat 2n
Tetraploid wheat 4n — Macaroni or durum wheat
DIPLOID wheat 2n
Modern bread wheat 6n

Active Learning

Activity

1. Explain the term hybridisation in the context of animal and plant breeding.
2. Find out more about selective breeding in pets or in livestock.
3. Design a 'super strawberry' – describe the properties that you think would be suitable.

Genetics and breeding

How is it that Labradors breed to make more Labradors, sweet peas make more of the same and amoebae make new amoebae? Why do we look a bit like each of our parents? These questions and many others relating to inheritance are explained by the science of genetics. The laws of genetics allow us to predict the possible outcomes from a mating between two parents.

The Labrador puppies look like their mother.

Inheritance

Some more about chromosomes and genes

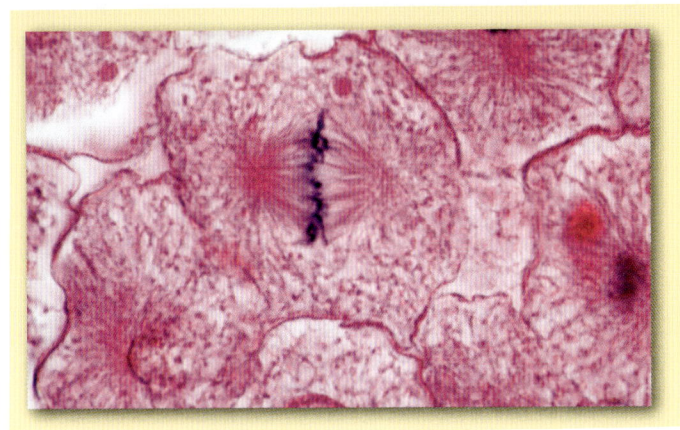

Each chromosome is a sequence of hundreds or even thousands of genes. Chromosomes are only visible during cell division. Most of the time they are spread throughout the nucleus. Between each division chromosomes carry out their main role and control the cell's work. This involves making enzymes and other proteins.

Remember that somatic cells contain two sets of chromosomes and a complete set of genes from each parent. Genes can lead to alternative appearances – blonde or brunette hair, blue or brown eyes, white or red flowers, the appearance or not of fruit fly wings. There are countless other examples in nature. Genes that can lead to alternative appearances in this way are referred to as **alleles**.

The big question in genetics is: *'What will the offspring look like?'*

The original experiments into genes and inheritance were carried out by an Austrian monk, Gregor Mendel. He experimented on pea plants over a 7-year period from 1856 to 1863. He observed that the pea plants had several varieties. The flowers could be purple or white, the seed coat could be smooth or wrinkled and the seeds' food store could be coloured yellow or green. The alternative form of each gene is called an allele.

Peas can be pollinated by insects. They can be artificially pollinated by a gardener or plant breeder. Here is what Mendel did to prevent self-pollination:

1. He grew 'true breeding' yellow- and green-coloured peas. (These had been grown for several generations.)

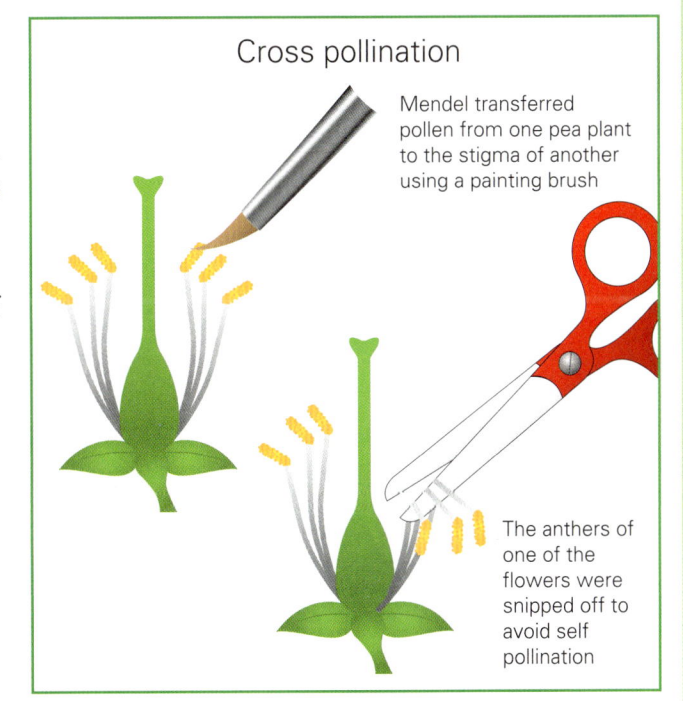

Cross pollination

Mendel transferred pollen from one pea plant to the stigma of another using a painting brush

The anthers of one of the flowers were snipped off to avoid self pollination

2. He cross-pollinated the flowers from each kind of plant – the ones that had grown from yellow- or from green-coloured seeds.

3. He collected the seeds from the pea pods and was surprised when he found that they were all coloured yellow.

Inheritance

Some more about chromosomes and genes

4 The following summer Mendel grew pea plants from those seeds and allowed self-pollination to take place.

5 When he harvested the seeds he got another surprise – three-quarters of the seeds were coloured yellow and a quarter of the seeds were green.

6 Mendel repeated his experiments with several different varieties of peas. His experiments were carried out with 29 000 plants.

Here is how Mendel explained how inheritance works:

Parents

True-breeding seeds only carry one form of the gene on their chromosomes – the yellow or green allele. These produce gametes that all carry the same allele, the one for yellow- or the one for green-coloured seeds.

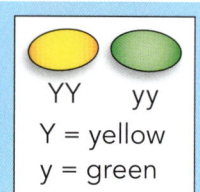

YY   yy
Y = yellow
y = green

First generation

Fertilisation following cross-pollination produces seeds that carry the allele from each parent and the adult plant produces yellow seeds. Mendel reasoned that yellow is **dominant** to green as far as seed colour is concerned.

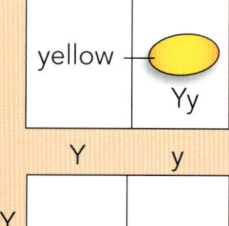

The seeds still contain the alleles for yellow and green seed colour and these appear in the gametes of the first generation. Mendel shows that self-pollination could lead to four **genotypes**. He used a Punnett Square to help the predictions.

yellow — Yy

Second generation

When the plants are self-pollinated and produce a second generation, they show proportions of offspring that are consistent with Mendel's predictions.

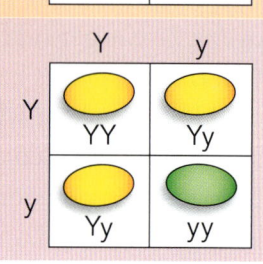

	Y	y
Y	YY	Yy
y	Yy	yy

Distinguishing phenotypes from genotypes

Every time you pass a reflective surface, you view your **phenotype** (fee-no-type) – your appearance. Your phenotype depends on the genes that you have inherited from your parents – your genotype (gee-no-type) – and the way that you have grown in a particular environment.

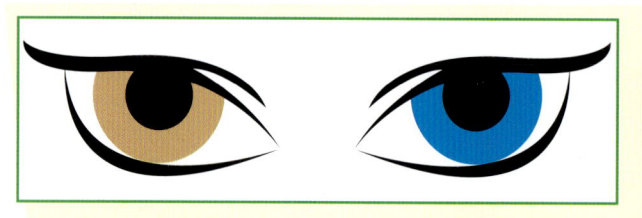

We inherit all our genes from our parents. Remember we have two sets of chromosomes and so have two sets of genes. Brown eyes and blue eyes are both examples of the phenotype for eye colour. Brown eye colour (B) is dominant to blue eye colour (b). The genotype, the combination of genes, contained in a brown-eyed person can be BB or Bb. The genes contained in a blue-eyed person can only be bb.

Inheritance

Before | After

Body-building through exercise can change your appearance. While exercise and a healthy diet can help body-builders to change their body, drugs can also be used to help the process but many of them have harmful effects on growth and blood pressure.

Active Learning

Activity

Prepare an illustrated classroom display to define each of the following terms that are used in genetics:

Allele   Haploid
Diploid   Heterozygous
Gamete   Homozygous
Genome   Phenotype
Genotypes   Somatic

An informative display should define the topic and provide suitable examples and illustrations. It should also make effective use of colour, texture, shape and pattern.

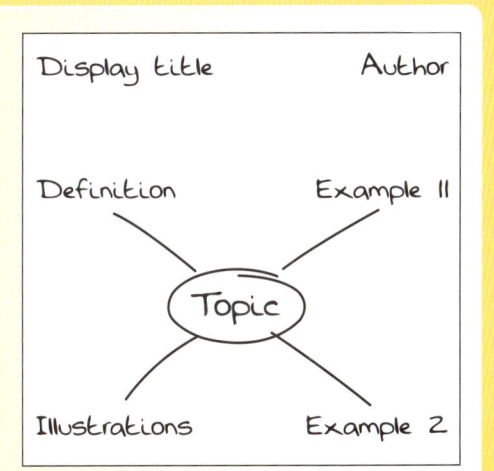

Breeding fruit for quality

Scottish scientists at Invergowrie in Perthshire have applied a modern twist to the production of new cross varieties of fruits such as raspberry. Although they use the same pollinating techniques as Mendel, they do not have to wait for several seasons to find out the genotypes of the offspring. They use gene profiling on seedlings to search for the best combinations of characteristics such as flavour, colour, disease resistance and nutritional qualities.

This raspberry has been developed using gene profiling.

Inheritance

Genetic counselling

👍 Genetics can help us to predict the phenotypes of individuals. Some mutations are harmful and can lead to inherited conditions and certain kinds of cancer.

Genetic counselling is offered to people with inherited conditions or those who might carry them when they want to have children. A genetic counsellor can calculate the risk of passing the condition on to the child. They will look at family histories and carry out ultrasound scans to look at the baby as it grows or perform tests on the mother's blood. Doctors can also collect the baby's cells from inside the womb so that these can be grown in the laboratory. They look for abnormalities and mutations in the chromosomes.

This couple is receiving genetic counselling.

Genetic counsellors will also calculate the risk of patients developing conditions. For example the gene BRCA1 (Breast Cancer Gene 1) was shown to suppress breast cancers. Women with mutations in the gene have a greater risk of developing breast cancer. Future counselling may include individual gene profiles – our own genetic map.

Mutation

Mutations are changes in the sequence of genes. Each **genome** contains huge numbers of mutations. Mutations create new combinations of genes or sequences of nucleotide bases. The process of evolution has been driven by mutations because they create new forms of genes. This is quite puzzling since we believe that most mutations are harmful. However mutations occasionally provide favourable characteristics to the offspring.

The X-Men were genetic mutants.

Mutations can be caused in a variety of ways. External **mutagens** (factors causing mutations) include viruses, chemicals and radiation. Mutations lead to changes in DNA or chromosomes. These mutations are passed on by the gametes.

Scientists believe that most mutations lead to small and insignificant changes to alleles. They carry out most of their research with micro-organisms.

Harmful mutations frequently result in cell death or poorly formed cells. Often they are unable to reproduce and those mutant genes leave the **gene pool**. Beneficial mutations lead to favourable physical or biochemical properties and these are passed on to the organism's offspring, enriching the gene pool.

Inheritance

Mutation

Beneficial mutations in humans

Sickle cell disease is an inherited condition that is found in tropical Africa where malaria is common. It is a fatal condition and sufferers are not expected to live beyond their 40s. Sickle cell disease affects the haemoglobin in red blood cells in people who carry the mutant gene on both sets of chromosomes (people who are **homozygous** for the sickle cell gene). People who are **heterozygous** for the gene, however, have been found to be more resistant to developing malaria.

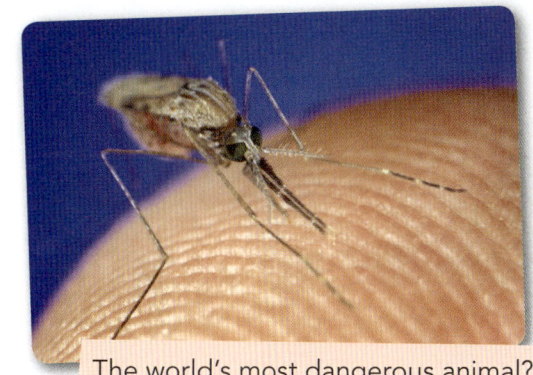

The world's most dangerous animal?

QUESTIONS

1. Use the words below to copy and complete the following sentences:

   one set   two sets   unpaired   paired

   Gametes include _____ of _____ chromosomes while the zygote contains _____ of _____ chromosomes.

2. Make a table that summarises the chromosome number and wheat varieties.

3. Find out more about Gregor Mendel. Who was he? Where did he live? Why was he interested in peas?

4. Explain why family histories are important when couples are thinking about having a baby.

GLOSSARY

Alleles Alternative forms of genes

Characteristics Refers to inherited traits, in other words the appearance and biochemical properties of an organism (for example hair colour, eye colour, the ability to make particular enzymes)

Dominant The allele that is displayed when two are present

Gamete Sex cell

Genetic counselling Professional healthcare advice

Heterozygous Carrying two different alleles

Hexaploid Six sets of chromosomes

Homozygous Carrying two identical alleles

Motile Able to move, for example sperm is moved by its tail

Ploidy The number of sets of chromosomes in a cell

Somatic Refers to diploid body cells

Tetraploid Four sets of chromosomes

MATERIALS
Earth's Materials

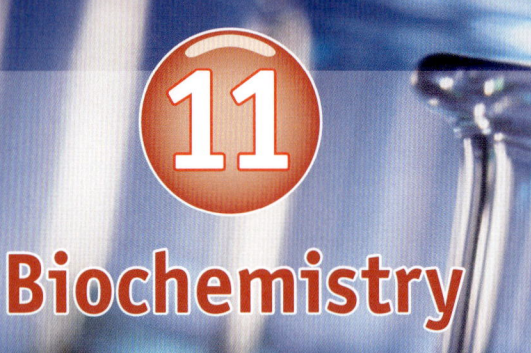

11 Biochemistry

Level 3 — What came before?

SCN 3-16a

I can differentiate between pure substances and mixtures in common use and can select appropriate physical methods for separating mixtures into their components.

SCN 3-17b

I can participate in practical activities to extract useful substances from natural resources.

Level 4 — What is this chapter about?

SCN 4-16a

I have carried out research into novel materials and can begin to explain the scientific basis of their properties and discuss the possible impacts they may have on society.

SCN 4-17a

I have explored how different materials can be derived from crude oil and their uses. I can explain the importance of carbon compounds in our lives.

Biochemistry

The chemistry of life

Biochemistry, the study of the chemistry which occurs in living things, depends on the versatile properties of carbon.

Introducing carbon

Carbon is one of the Earth's most abundant elements. It combines with other elements to form a huge number of compounds, and many are found in living things. Carbon is found in carbohydrates, lipids and proteins, making it an essential element for sustaining life on the planet.

Carbon occurs naturally in a variety of forms. Charcoal, graphite and diamond are all made of the element carbon.

Carbohydrates

Carbohydrates are found throughout all living things. They are mainly used as a source of energy and as structural scaffolding in cells.

Carbohydrates, also called '**saccharides**', contain the elements carbon (C), hydrogen (H) and oxygen (O). The simplest arrangement present in plants and animals are called **monosaccharides**, for example the simple sugar glucose. Glucose is a soluble carbohydrate and is the raw material for cellular respiration. Glucose can be built into larger carbohydrate molecules.

Maltose is a **disaccharide** – it contains two sugar units. Cellulose, starch and glycogen are **polysaccharides** formed by many glucose molecules.

Lactose is a disaccharide that is found in milk. Lactose is formed from glucose and galactose.

Sucrose (table sugar) is a disaccharide that can be purified from a variety of plants, such as sugar beet and sugar cane. Sucrose is formed from glucose and fructose.

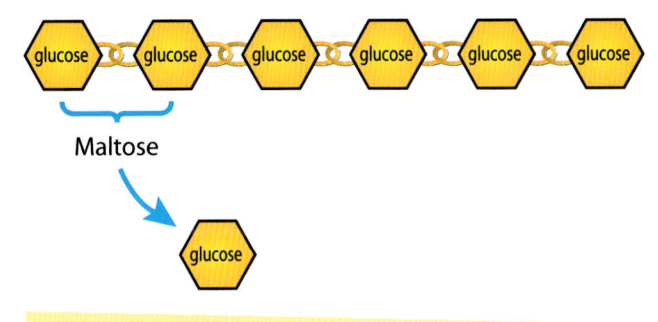

Starch
(stored carbohydrate in plants)

Starch is a larger carbohydrate molecule made up of many smaller glucose molecules linked together.

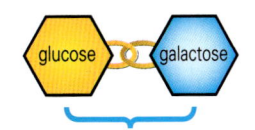

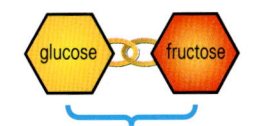

89

Biochemistry

Carbohydrates

Carbohydrates in plants

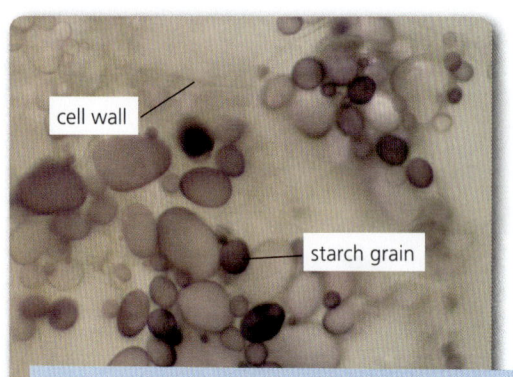

The cellulose cell wall and starch grains are visible in these potato cells.

In plants, glucose is used for respiration and is also converted into other carbohydrates such as cellulose and starch. Cell walls are composed of cellulose, making it an essential structural material in plants. Excess glucose is converted to starch, an insoluble molecule, providing a food store for the plant.

> **Active Learning**
>
> **Activity**
>
> Examine fibres in fresh plant materials and in plant products such as cotton and paper.
>
> Use iodine solution (take care) to test a range of materials for the presence of starch.

Carbohydrates in animals

In animals, carbohydrate obtained from the diet is digested to provide glucose for cellular respiration. This provides energy for cell division, movement, heat generation and to sustain essential biochemical reactions. Excess glucose is converted to insoluble glycogen which can be stored in muscles and liver tissue.

Lipids

Lipids, like carbohydrates, also contain the elements carbon, hydrogen and oxygen. Lipids include fats, oils and waxes. All these substances are **hydrophobic** – they do not like water. They are useful at creating waterproof barriers in living systems and have a significant role to play in the structure of cells. In addition, they provide energy reserves.

Fats and oils

Fats and oils are lipids. They are made up of a molecule of glycerol which is attached to three fatty acids. The composition of the fatty acids can vary which results in differences in the properties of fats and oils, such as melting point and energy value. Generally 'fats' are lipids that are solid at room temperature and 'oils' are liquid at room temperature.

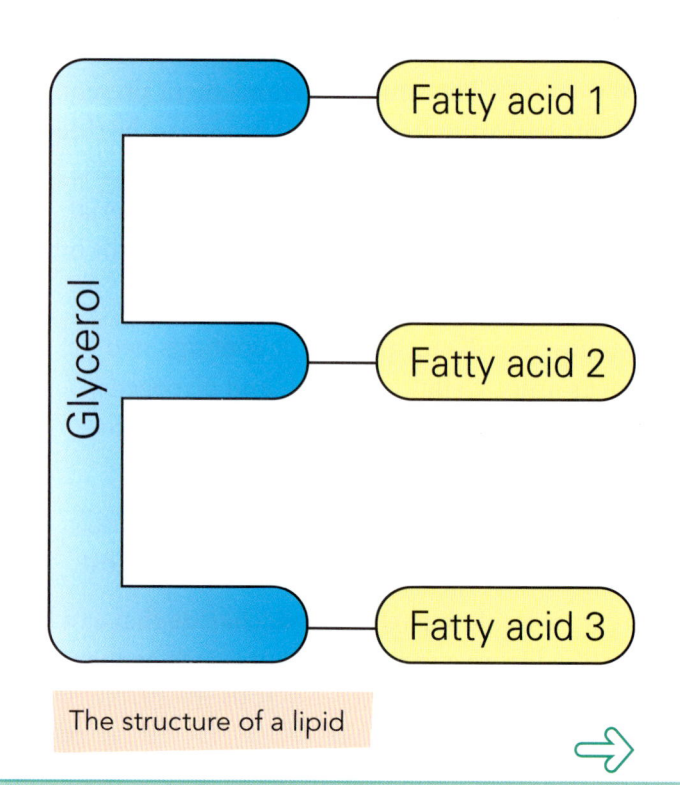

The structure of a lipid

Biochemistry

Lipids

Lipids and living things

Lipids are effective energy stores; they can store twice the energy of carbohydrates. This energy is released in the process of respiration. Carbohydrates can be converted into lipids for long-term storage.

In animals, this lipid is stored in **adipose** tissue. This tissue provides thermal insulation and protection of parts of the body.

In plants, the conversion of excess carbohydrate into lipid, usually in the form of oils, allows for a greater energy store in a limited space.

Lipids are important chemicals that play an essential role in all the membranes that are found surrounding cells and inside cells.

Waxes

Both plants and animals manufacture **waxes**. Being water-repellent, they form effective barriers providing protection for hair, skin and feathers in animals and preventing water loss or attack from parasitic organisms in plants. Examples of wax produced by living things include beeswax, earwax, lanolin on sheep's wool and the waterproof covering of leaves.

This honeycomb is built from beeswax.

A baby seal can have equal masses of muscle and adipose fat. The adipose tissue helps to keep it warm in low temperatures.

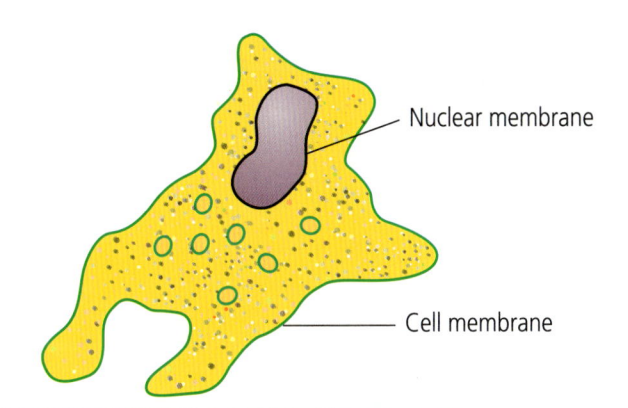

Membranes are made from lipids and proteins. They are able to control the passage of materials into the cell and each part of it.

Active Learning

Activity

Research one of the following using library or Internet resources:

Examples of foods that are high in lipid content **OR**

'Saturated' and 'unsaturated' dietary fats **OR**

Cholesterol in the human body.

Write up your findings in a short report.

91

Biochemistry

Proteins

Proteins are also built from carbon, hydrogen and oxygen. In addition, however, proteins always contain nitrogen and small proportions of sulphur. CHONS atoms are arranged into molecules called **amino acids**. There are twenty naturally-occurring amino acids.

The table below shows a list of amino acids and their common abbreviations.

Alanine	Ala	Leucine	Leu
Arginine	Arg	Lysine	Lys
Asparagine	Asn	Methionine	Met
Aspartic acid	Asp	Phenylalanine	Phe
Cysteine	Cys	Proline	Pro
Glutamic acid	Glu	Serine	Ser
Glutamine	Gln	Threonine	Thr
Glycine	Gly	Tryptophan	Trp
Histidine	His	Tyrosine	Tyr
Isoleucine	Ile	Valine	Val

Amino acids are joined together in chains to form polypeptides; this is the primary structure of a protein molecule.

Proteins are built from chains of the twenty naturally-occurring amino acids. These are combined into a huge variety of amino acid sequences. Each protein is made from a precise sequence of amino acids. The code for each protein is determined by a gene in the chromosomes.

Amino acid sequence is coded in nuclear DNA. If an error exists in the DNA then the amino acid sequence will be incorrect and the protein will be affected. This is a mutation.

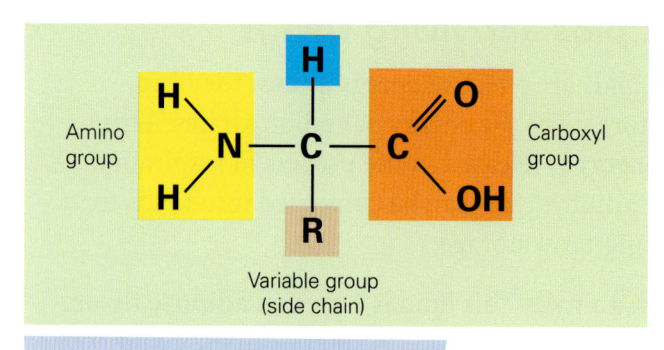

The structure of an amino acid

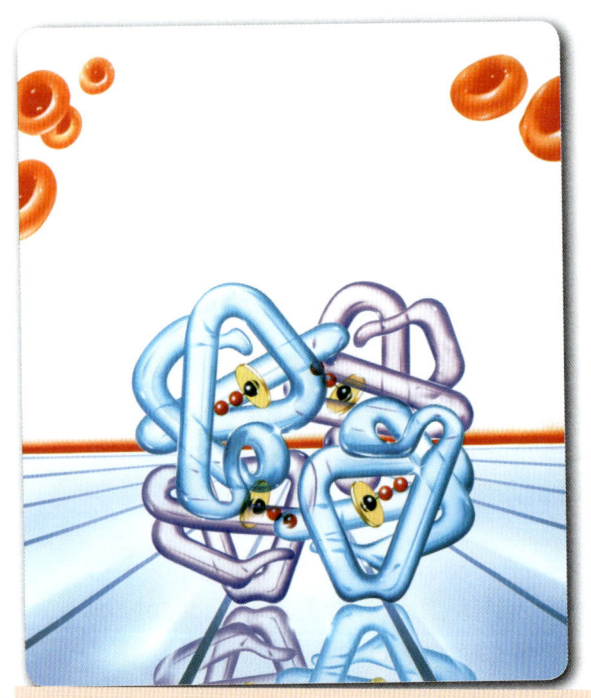

A protein molecule's structure becomes much more complicated when polypeptide chains are put together, folded and twisted, so that additional bonding occurs between amino acids.

Biochemistry

Proteins and living things

Proteins are used in many different ways within living organisms. They perform many structural and functional roles in all living systems. Some of these are summarised in the table below.

Type of protein	Function	Examples
Structural	Support	Spider silk, feathers, bone, cell membranes
Storage	Supply amino acids	Casein (milk protein) supplies amino acids for growing baby mammals
Transporter	Move substances	Haemoglobin and oxygen transport
Hormonal	Co-ordinating activities	Insulin helps control sugar balance
Contractile	Movement	Muscle proteins
Defensive	Act against infection	Antibodies
Enzymic	Control chemical reactions	Digestive enzymes for chemical breakdown. Synthetic enzymes needed to build new cellular material

Protein metabolism

In extreme circumstances, such as starvation, proteins can be broken down to release energy for an organism. Tissue proteins are so valuable that their loss will have negative effects on the appearance and **metabolism** of the organism and will seriously affect its long-term survival.

Biopolymers

Polymers are 'giant' molecules made up of long chains of building block molecules. For example, starch and cellulose are polymers that are made from lots of glucose molecules; proteins are polymers that are made from amino acids.

Synthetic (man-made) polymers, such as polyethylene, nylon and polyurethane, are the basis of the plastics industry and they have many commercial uses. The problem is that these polymers are non-biodegradable and are difficult to break down. They will persist in the environment for many centuries. They are manufactured from fossil fuels.

Naturally-occurring polymers are the main parts of biological materials like leather, fur, wool, silk, cellulose and plant fibres.

Biochemistry

Biopolymers

Biopolymers have important roles in nature. DNA, proteins, fatty acids and starch are biopolymers involved with controlling the structure and functions of living things and supplying energy.

Biopolymers manufactured by living organisms include soya proteins, cellulose and starch.

Prior to 1940, a process to manufacture bioplastic car parts from protein extracted from soya beans was being developed by the Ford Motor Company. The onset of the Second World War halted the development. Since the 1960s, however, biopolymer research has greatly increased.

Cellulose is a structural carbohydrate which is found in plant cell walls. Cellulose is made of long chains of glucose molecules and is the most common biopolymer. It makes up more than 30% of all plant material.

Paper, cotton and linen contain high proportions of cellulose, a fibrous polymer.

Starch is a polymer of glucose molecules. It is a carbohydrate that is found throughout the plant kingdom. Potatoes, wheat and rice are examples of staple crops that are grown to provide starch, and therefore energy, to people. Glycogen is the polymer of glucose that is found stored in animal muscle and the liver.

Bioplastics manufactured by living organisms

Arabidopsis (A-rah-bid-op-sis), a member of the mustard family, is widely used in plant science research. It has been genetically engineered using the genes from a bacterium that can manufacture the plastic PHBV (polyhydroxybutyrate-valerate).

Arabidopsis thaliana

PHBV plastic can be moulded into shapes, such as plastic bags or razors, and can biodegrade back into carbon dioxide and water.

Arabidopsis has only five chromosomes. Its complete genetic makeup (its **genome**) has been identified using the same techniques as were used for the Human Genome Project. It is an ideal plant for experiments since it completes its life cycle in only 6 weeks. After the plant is harvested the plastic is dissolved in a solvent. The plastic is then separated from the solvent by distillation.

The production of bioplastics offers exciting opportunities for the future. Their production reduces the use of fossil fuels but will put additional pressure on land and water resources and food production. In the future it may be possible to genetically engineer a plant to produce plastics specifically in its stem and leaves. The fruits and seeds of the plant would contain no plastic and remain edible.

Biochemistry

Biopolymers in medicine

Synthetic biopolymers can be used in the human body, as the body's immune system does not reject them. One medical use of biopolymers is in the coating of capsules containing medicines.

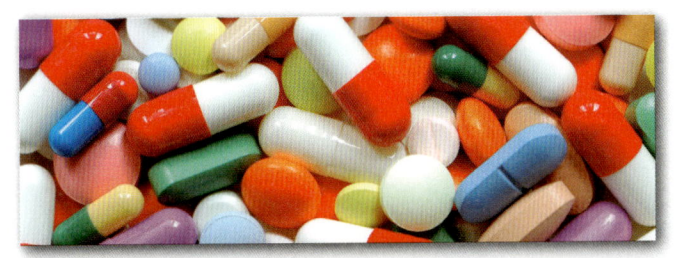

Biopolymers are also being used as replacement parts in the body. Such replacement parts as artificial corneas, lenses, tendons, ligaments, joints, pacemakers, heart valves and stents can be manufactured from durable biopolymers.

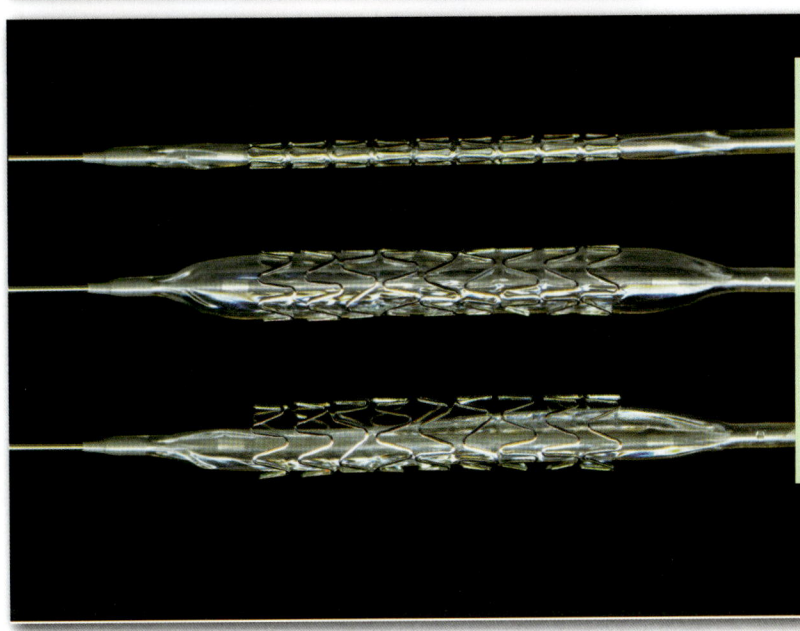

It's just like magic! Surgeons pass the stent in a tube called a catheter through the patient's blood vessels, inflate the balloon to open and support the vessel, and then remove the catheter and balloon. The stent is left behind to keep the damaged blood vessel open.

Natural fibres such as alginates (from seaweeds), chitin (from the external skeletons of insects) and keratin (hair and nails) are biopolymers. Alginate fibres are used in wound dressings. They form a gel when in contact with blood. This gel keeps the surface of the wound moist and aids the healing process.

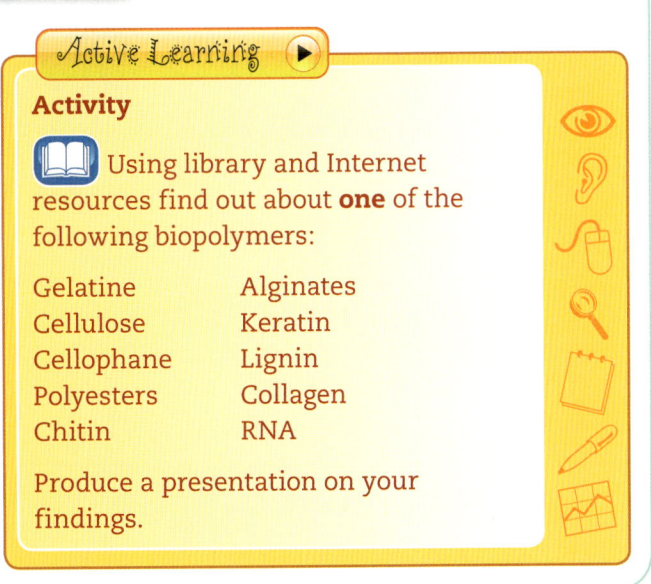

Active Learning

Activity

Using library and Internet resources find out about **one** of the following biopolymers:

Gelatine	Alginates
Cellulose	Keratin
Cellophane	Lignin
Polyesters	Collagen
Chitin	RNA

Produce a presentation on your findings.

95

Biochemistry

QUESTIONS

1. Make a table to summarise the biochemical groups carbohydrates, proteins and lipids. Include information about their composition, their structure and the occurrence of each group.
2. Find out why excess glucose must be stored in insoluble forms in both plants and animals.
3. Suggest why glycogen would be stored specifically in muscle and liver tissue.
4. Match the statements about examples of particular protein functions.

1	Build up reactions	A	Protein digestion
2	Provide amino acids	B	Bone protein
3	Movement	C	Blood proteins
4	Transport carbon dioxide	D	Muscle proteins
5	Provide support	E	Antibodies
6	Act against infection	F	Metabolism

5. Explain the difference between synthetic polymers and biopolymers.
6. Explain in your own words, as fully as you can, the following sentence: 'Synthetic polymers will persist in the environment for many centuries.'
7. Explain the following sentence in your own words: 'The production of bioplastics reduces the use of fossil fuels but will put additional pressure on land and water resources and food production.'

GLOSSARY

Amino acids Building blocks for protein

Metabolism All the cell's chemical and physical processes

Polymer Large molecule made from repeating basic units

Saccharides Carbohydrate sugar molecules

Index

A
abiotic factors 9
acid rain 37, 39
adaptation 14–16
adipose tissue 50, 91
aerobic respiration 9
   investigations 29–34
aestivation 54–5
agriculture 11–12
alcohol industry 66
algae 12–13
algal blooms 12–13
alleles 83, 86
amino acids 11, 92, 93
anaerobic digestion 40
anaerobic respiration 30
animal behaviour 52–7
animal behaviour scientists 56
animal life cycles 73–6
animals, carbohydrates 90
antibiotics 68
Arabidopsis 94
Artemia salina (brine shrimps) 73–6
artificial plant propagation 25–6
asexual reproduction 73
atmosphere 36

B
bacterial industries 68–9
baking industry 67
bees 47, 52
behaviour 52–7
behavioural adaptation 14
binary fission 73
biochemistry 89–95
biodiesel 40
biogas 40
biological indicators 41–2
biological washing powders 69
biomass 39
biopolymers 93–5
biorenewables 39–41
biotechnology 66–71
biotic factors 9
bivalent chromosomes 59
blastocysts 60
blood cells 62–3
blood pressure 48
blood stem cells 63
body-building 85
bones, repair of broken 62
brains 48, 49, 50
bread making 67
brewing 66
brine shrimps (*Artemia salina*) 73–6
bulbs 25

C
camouflage 55
carbohydrates 89–90
carbon 89
carbon capture and storage (CCS) 39
carbon cycle 9
carbon dioxide (CO_2) 9, 36, 39
carpel 8, 21
CCS (carbon capture and storage) 39
cell division 59–60
cell growth 59–64
cell repair 59–64
cellular respiration 90
cellulose 90, 94
cheese production 68
choice chambers 56
chromosomes 59, 79, 81–4
climate change 37, 39, 42
clones 26
CO_2 (carbon dioxide) 9, 36, 39
coal 36, 38
cold-blooded animals 47
colour adaptation 15
combustion 36–7
control centres 45, 46, 48
courtship rituals 56
cows 13
cystic fibrosis 70–1
cysts 73–4

D
daffodils 25
Darwin, Charles 14
data collection 42
decomposition 10, 11
defence mechanisms 55
dehydration 48
denitrification 11
deoxyribonucleic acid (DNA) 79, 92, 94
differentiation, and vegetative propagation 26
diploid cells 81
disaccharides 89
distilling 66
division, plant propagation 26
DNA (deoxyribonucleic acid) 79, 92, 94
DNA profiling 80
dormancy 23

E
effectors 45, 47
electricity generation 38
embryos 60, 64
emigration 17
endocrine glands 49
enzymes 66, 69–70
ethanol 40
eutrophication 12–13
evolution 14
exercise, and respiration 29–30
external fertilisation 73
eye colour 84

F
fats 91
fatty acids 91, 94
fertilisation 8, 73
fertilisers 11–12
flowers 21
food chains 7
food industry 68
food webs 7
fossil fuels 36–9, 93
Frisch, Karl von 56
fruit breeding 85

G
gametes 73, 81, 86
gas 36, 38
gene profiling 85
gene therapy 70–1
genes 79–80
genetic code 59
genetic counselling 86

Index

genetic fingerprinting 80
genetics 82–6
genomes 86
genotypes 84
germination 22–3
global warming 37
glucagon 49
glucose 89, 90
glucose balance 49–50
glycerol 91
greenhouse effect 37
growth, animal 60

H
habitat destruction 38
haploid cells 81
hibernation 15, 54
human population 17–18
humans
   blood cells 62
   genes 79–80
   genetic code 59
   glucose balance 49–50
   repair of tissues 61–2
   temperature control 46–7
   water balance 48
hydrophobic substances 91
hydroponics 23
hypothalmus 48

I
immigration 17
indicator species 41
inheritance 79–87
innate behaviour 52
instinctive behaviour 52
insulin 49
interdependence 7–14
internal fertilisation 73

L
lactose 89
learning 54
lichens 41
life expectancy 18
lipids 90–1
Lorenz, Konrad 56

M
malaria 13
medicine 68, 69–70, 95
Mendel, Gregor 83–4

meristems 61
metabolism 47, 93
methane 37
microclimates 9
micropropagation 26
migration 52, 55
mineral cycle 10
monosaccharides 89
mutagens 86
mutations 86–7, 92

N
nano-biotechnology 71
nanotechnology 71
natural gas 36, 38
natural hazards 18
nerves 48
nitrification 11
nitrogen cycle 11
nuclei 59

O
oil (fossil fuel) 36, 38
oil spills 38
oils (lipids) 91
optimum 45
orang-utans 19

P
parasites 13–14
peat 36
pharmacy industries 68–9
PHBV (polyhydroxybutyrate-valerate) 94
phenology 42
phenotypes 84
photosynthesis 7, 33–4
physiological adaptation 15
physiological control 45–50
plant growth 24, 61
plant propagation 21–6
plants, carbohydrates 90
plastics industry 93
ploidy 82
pollination 8, 21, 83–4
polyhydroxybutyrate-valerate (PHBV) 94
polymers 93
polyploidy 82
polysaccharides 89
population growth 16–19
potatoes 25

power stations 38–9
propagation, plant 21–6
protein metabolism 93
proteins 92–3, 94

R
receptors 45
red blood cells 62–3
renewable energy sources 39–41
reproduction 73–6
reproductive adaptation 15
respiration 29–34, 90
runners (stolons) 25

S
saccharides 89
scientists, animal behaviour 56
seasonal indicators 42
seasonal migration 17
seed dispersal 8
seeds 21–3
sexual reproduction 73, 81
shellfish 13
shelter 9
sickle cell disease 87
silage 68
skin tissue repair 61
SO_2 (sulphur dioxide) 41
somatic cells 81, 83
spider plants 25
stamen 8, 21
starch 89, 90, 94
stem cells 63–4
stem cuttings 26
stolons (runners) 25
structural adaptation 16
sucrose 89
sulphur dioxide (SO_2) 41
survival, and animal behaviour 54–6
symbiosis 13–14
syngas 40

T
temperature control
   in animals 47
   in humans 46–7
theory of evolution 14
thyroid gland 49
Tinbergen, Nikolaas 56
training animals 53
tubers 25

Index

U
urine production 48

V
vegetative processes, of plant propagation 24–6
von Frisch, Karl 56

W
warm-blooded animals 47
washing powders, biological 69
water balance 48
waxes 91
white blood cells 62
wood, as biomass 40–1

Y
yeast industries 66–7
yoghurt 68

Z
zygotes 74, 81

Curriculum for Excellence mapping grid

			1	2	3	4	5	6	7	8	9	10	11
Curriculum for Excellence Science Level 4 Experiences and Outcomes	Planet Earth	SCN 4-01a	■										
		SCN 4-02a		■									
		SCN 4-02b			■								
		SCN 4-03a	■										
		SCN 4-04a				■							
		SCN 4-04b				■							
		SCN 4-05a											
		SCN 4-05b											
		SCN 4-06a											
	Forces, Electricity and Waves	SCN 4-07a											
		SCN 4-07b											
		SCN 4-08a											
		SCN 4-08b											
		SCN 4-09a											
		SCN 4-09b											
		SCN 4-09c											
		SCN 4-10a											
		SCN 4-10b											
		SCN 4-11a											
		SCN 4-11b											
	Biological Systems	SCN 4-12a					■						
		SCN 4-12b						■					
		SCN 4-13a							■				
		SCN 4-13b								■			
		SCN 4-13c											
		SCN 4-14a									■		
		SCN 4-14b		■							■		
		SCN 4-14c										■	
	Materials	SCN 4-15a											
		SCN 4-16a											■
		SCN 4-16b											
		SCN 4-17a											■
		SCN 4-18a				■							
		SCN 4-19a											
		SCN 4-19b											
	Topical Science	SCN 4-20a											
		SCN 4-20b											
		Chapter	1	2	3	4	5	6	7	8	9	10	11